THE
MAKING OF AMERICA
SERIES

EDGECOMBE COUNTY
ALONG THE TAR RIVER

Miss Mamie Ruffin was about 20 in the early 1900s when this photo was made by Sidney Rufus Alley. Alley came to Tarboro in the 1880s to operate a photography studio and was quite successful in preserving hundreds of images of the growth of Tarboro and its families. Ruffin married Ben Lawrence and is remembered for her fine needlework in various clothing items at the Blount-Bridgers House Museum, including extremely detailed smocking on a christening gown. She died in 1953 and is buried in the Lawrence Cemetery near Battleboro. (Courtesy of Blount-Bridgers House Archives.)

THE
MAKING OF AMERICA
SERIES

EDGECOMBE COUNTY
ALONG THE TAR RIVER

MONIKA S. FLEMING

ARCADIA

Published by Arcadia Publishing,
an imprint of Tempus Publishing, Inc.
2 Cumberland Street
Charleston, SC 29401

Printed in Great Britain.

Library of Congress Catalog Card Number: 2002114923

For all general information contact Arcadia Publishing at:
Telephone 843-853-2070
Fax 843-853-0044
E-Mail sales@arcadiapublishing.com

For customer service and orders:
Toll-Free 1-888-313-2665

Visit us on the Internet at http://www.arcadiapublishing.com

Front cover: *Students at Leggett School in township No. 5 were transported to school in mule-drawn wagons until school buses became available in the 1930s. (Courtesy of Edgecombe County Memorial Library.)*

4

CONTENTS

ACKNOWLEDGMENTS

Several friends and professional colleagues have contributed time, energy, and special efforts to help me complete this book. I would like to thank each of them. Eric Blevins of the North Carolina Museum of History for photographs. Edward Lewis and Donald Morris for contributing personal photographs. Mr. and Mrs. Edward Warren of South Carolina for donating information about the Spanish American War. Joan Pollack of Pennsylvania for getting me started on the research of the Jewish immigrants, and for sharing her family records. Marcia Chesson for checking some of the manuscript. David Gammon for assisting with some family histories. Betty Reason, president of the Edgecombe County Genealogical Society, for research information and encouragement. Steve Massengill, photo archivist at the North Carolina Office of Archives and History in Raleigh, for helping me select photos and getting them to me so quickly. The many students who asked questions about local history, and who brought stories to class that encouraged my research. Traci Thompson, local history librarian at the Edgecombe County Memorial Library, for checking dates and facts and providing photos from the library collection. Nancy Boykin, an excellent student, and her daughter Tina were a tremendous help with research and last-minute details. The wonderful staff of the Blount-Bridgers House: Carol Banks and Eric Greene for help with photographs; and especially Director Meade Horne for proofreading the manuscript and making suggestions. Cue Fleming, my father-in-law, for editorial suggestions. Finally, my husband Martin Fleming for helping gather photos and information for the chapter on the Civil War and for locating information on World War II.

INTRODUCTION

Edgecombe County is located in northeastern North Carolina on the western edge of the coastal plain. It is about 75 miles east of Raleigh and just over 110 miles from the Atlantic Ocean. It is one of the state's earliest settlements and has a rich agricultural history that expanded into industry in the late nineteenth century, as the region was rebuilding after the Civil War. The county also has been home to state and national leaders in the military and in politics, and has produced several acclaimed artists and writers. While some individuals stand out, most residents are average people whose lifestyles nonetheless produce the interesting community that is the story of this book.

The county seat of Tarboro is one of the ten oldest towns in North Carolina. The name comes from the river that flows through the area. There were different pronounciations of the river's name—possibly a Tuscaroran word meaning health—from "Tar" to "Tau." These contributed to the various spellings of the town's name: Tarborough and Tarrburg in the 1760s, Tawborough in the mid-nineteenth century, and Tarboro today. What began as a 1-square-mile area with fewer than 20 families is today a town of over 12,000. The town common, which originally surrounded the town, is the second oldest legislated common in the United States. Now near the center of town, it remains the location of patriotic and cultural celebrations.

Several other towns and crossroad communities have sprung up around this county of over 500 square miles. In its western part, three urban areas—Whitakers, Rocky Mount, and Sharpsburg—are divided between two counties with a railroad track as county line with Nash County. Fishing Creek serves as the county line along the northeastern boundary with Halifax County; the communities in this area include Lawrence and Speed. To the east is Martin County and to the southeast is Pitt County. The southern communities, home to some of the area's early settlers, include Old Sparta and Crisp. The railroad created the towns of Conetoe, Pinetops, and Macclesfield. Wilson County on the southwest border was once a part of Edgecombe County. With the exception of Rocky Mount—a regional urban center of over 60,000 inhabitants—all communities are rural with populations ranging from a couple hundred to a couple thousand. Across the Tar River from

In 1882, this map of Tarboro was produced by the O.W. Gray & Son Company of Philadelphia. It clearly identifies the residents and businesses in town, and shows the expansion of town north and west of the original boundaries. Original copies of this map hang in the Edgecombe County Memorial Library and in the Pender Museum.

Tarboro is Princeville, the oldest African-American incorporated town in the United States.

Edgecombe County's population has been a mixture of European settlers and Africans since the eighteenth century. By 1860, African Americans outnumbered whites, as they still do today—although the population in all towns except Princeville is now about equal between those races. In the last decade, the Hispanic population has been growing faster than the white or African-American. There is also a small percentage of Asian Americans in the county.

The land produces various crops: cotton, tobacco, peanuts, corn, and soybeans are still profitable today. Pine forests provided the raw material for naval stores in the past. Other products include poultry and swine. The oldest industry in the county was a textile mill that began in 1818 and continued operation until 1996. Twentieth-century industries produced mattresses, rugs, caskets, farm equipment, electric transformers, power tools, plastics, work gloves, and clothing. The largest structure in the county today is the QVC distribution center that opened in 2000.

The Tar River flowing through the county has forever changed its landscape and people. It has nourished the land, provided a trade route, and offered entertainment from fishing to skating in various seasons. The land around the river is rich in nutrients and produces good crops. The river was also the major transportation route for the first 200 years of European settlement. Although the first railroad track was placed in the county in 1840, it was not until 50 years later that the steam locomotive began to replace steamboats for getting goods to market. The river and some of it tributaries also were used for baptisms. However, even with all its benefits, the river also reminds citizens of the devastating power of nature. Floods have been recorded since the 1780s: they may not occur for 50 years or more, or they may appear every decade. The elevation of most of the county is approximately 50 feet, leaving it at great risk. The flood of 1958 caused the low-lying town of Princeville to build a dike. In 1999, Edgecombe County and much of eastern North Carolina experienced the "Flood of the Century" following Hurricane Floyd. Over 40 percent of Tarboro and much of the county was underwater. The towns of Speed, Princeville, and Old Sparta were completely underwater. Still, as throughout history, the flood waters receded and the people recovered.

Communities were growing all over Edgecombe county in the 1880s. The Benjamin Eagles House was probably constructed during this period in Crisp, a town that had been settled since the Revolutionary War. The Eagles family operated a store at the crossroads, which is still run by Eagles's descendents today.

Two previous histories of Edgecombe County have been written. In 1920, J. Kelly Turner and John Luther Bridgers Jr. wrote a detailed local history. However, that work focuses on the upper middle class. While it does include information about history, politics, and religious developments, much is missing—especially since it predates most of the twentieth century. Professor Alan Watson's *Edgecombe County: A Brief History* was published in the late 1970s. While it covers more of the twentieth century and much political history, it is only a quarter the length of Turner and Bridgers's book. In the 1990s, two pictorial histories displayed the area's rich heritage preserved in photographs and oral histories.

Still, much history has yet to be told—stories of strong women, tales of brave soldiers, accounts of innovative businessmen, and descriptions of events that shaped the county and its residents. This is the purpose of this volume. It does not seek to replace those that have come before, but to enrich our awareness of county heritage.

Lawrence and Sallie Barnes Fountain family of the Leggett community posed for S.R. Alley. Their son Lawrence H. Fountain became a leading politician from North Carolina, serving 30 years in the United States Congress. (Courtesy of North Carolina Office of Archives and History.)

1. LIFE ALONG THE RIVER IN THE EIGHTEENTH CENTURY

The Tar River begins as a spring in present-day Person County. It meanders south and east for 180 miles through eastern North Carolina before it merges with the Pamlico River near Washington, North Carolina, and flows into the Pamlico Sound. Approximately 75 miles of the Tar flows through present-day Edgecombe County. Together with its tributaries—Town Creek in the south, Swift Creek in the northwest, and Fishing Creek along the northeast—this waterway was the early transportation route for the Native Americans who lived in this area since the fifteenth century. The Tuscarora tribe camped along its banks, and the Tar provided both food and a water route for trade with other tribes throughout the state.

Surveyor and explorer John Lawson may have visited the area as early as 1701, during his exploration through the backwoods of North and South Carolina. In his journal *A New Voyage to Carolina*, he does not mention the Tar River, but does refer to the Pampticough River (modern-day Pamlico) and describes the natives:

> We had not gone past two Miles, e're we met with about 500 Tuskeruros in one Hunting-Quarter. They had made themselves Streets of Houses, built with Pine bark, not with round Tops, as they commonly use, but Ridge Fashion, after the manner of most other Indians. We got nothing amongst them but Corn, Flesh being not plentiful, by reason of the great Number of their People.

In 1663, King Charles of England granted eight Lords Proprietors title to all the land south of Virginia and north of Florida, calling it Carolina. Although the first Carolina settlers migrated along the rivers of Charleston, by the early 1700s people were moving inland. Many moved south from Virginia into the northern coastal plains along the Roanoke and Tar Rivers. Others moved upriver from the coastal communities of Bath and New Bern. In 1710, some Swiss settlers occupied the Neuse River basin. These settlers began encroaching on the land of the native Tuscarora, who suffered a smallpox epidemic in the spring of 1711. In retaliation for this epidemic and other grievances, the southern Tuscaroras

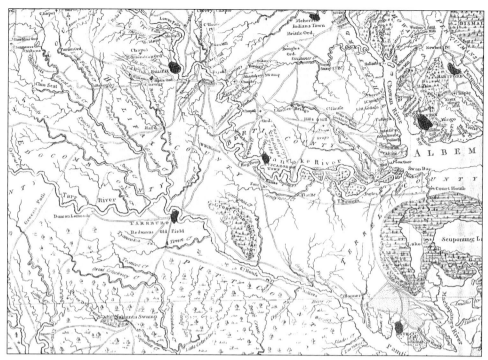

The Collett Map of 1770 is the first Carolina map to show Tarboro (Tarrburg) and Edgecombe County. Notice the Tarr River with its various tributaries, including Town Creek, where the earliest settlers lived. Redman's Old Field was the site of the courthouse. (Courtesy of North Carolina Office of Archives and History.)

launched an attack and massacred over 100 settlers in the New Bern area in September of that year. During the next three years, local militia supported by South Carolina troops fought the Native Americans. Captured Tuscaroras were sold into slavery, while some survivors left the area to join the Iroquois Confederacy. This Tuscarora War resulted in displacing most of the natives and opening the way for Europeans to migrate inland and settle along the rivers and creeks by the late 1720s.

Also in 1729, seven of the Lords Proprietors sold their land back to the King because they were not earning the expected income from settlers. This changed the proprietary colony of North Carolina (by then separated from South Carolina) into a royal colony subject to English rule. The eighth proprietor, Lord Granville, chose to keep his share and was granted one-eighth of the original land grant: the northern area of North Carolina that bordered Virginia. This contributed to disputes over who actually owned the land and to whom taxes should be paid—the Crown or Lord Granville.

The earliest reference to the Tar River is on the Moseley Map of 1733, which clearly identifies Edgecombe Precinct as the western settlement of the Albemarle region. The precinct extended roughly southwest from the banks of the Roanoke

River to the banks of the Neuse River, and northwest to the Virginia line surveyed in 1728. The area was approximately ten times larger than the 511 square miles of the present-day county. It is estimated that before 1730, no more than 20 families lived along the river in what was part of Bertie County and is now Edgecombe County. Colonial records give various dates for the political recognition of this area, ranging from 1732 to 1741. Deeds and land grants indicate that settlers inhabited the area as early as 1730. The *Colonial Records of North Carolina* listed 65 individuals in "arrears of Quit Rents" in Edgecombe Precinct in March 1732. Some of the landowners listed in the records have descendants in the area today: Bryans, Braswell, Davis, Fort, Hall, Jones, Jenkins, Lewis, Lane, O'Neal, Pope, Smith, Taylor, Turner, Williams, and Whitehead.

Royal Governor Burrington created Edgecombe Precinct in 1732, appointed justices of the peace, and ordered quarterly precinct courts. The precinct was named in honor of Lord Richard Edgecombe, an English nobleman. Even though the governor had followed appropriate procedures, some members of the general assembly protested that only the Assembly could create a new precinct, and thus refused to recognize its representatives. In 1734, a bill was introduced to create Edgecombe County. It did not pass, despite the presence of

The Tar River winds through Edgecombe County from the western boundary with Nash County, passes through the middle of the county, and crosses the southeast corner adjoining Pitt County. Early settlers lived along the river banks or its creeks. (Courtesy of Edgecombe County Memorial Library.)

seated representatives. The status of Edgecombe was not established until 1741, when the general assembly finally recognized Edgecombe as the 14th county in the colony.

The new county used the original's boundaries and consisted of approximately 4,100 square miles or over 2 million acres. All of that available land soon attracted more settlers from southern Virginia as well as those coming upriver from the coast. Land records indicate the county received a population influx from the late 1740s through the 1750s. Within just a few years, Edgecombe became the most populated county in the colony with a population of over 10,000.

Hundreds of settlers arrived and purchased land near the Tar River or one of its tributaries. Holdings ranged from 100 to 800 acres per purchase, with 350 acres being average. Elisha Battle moved from Southside Virginia in 1747 and settled along the Tar River near present-day Rocky Mount, about 16 miles west of Tarboro. Battle soon acquired more land and extended his farm to the Falls of the River. Battle was very active in the political development of this county. He began as a Justice of the Peace, an office that he would hold for almost 40 years. He served as a commissioner in the creation of Tarboro. During the Revolution, he was a representative to the colonial assembly, chairman of the committee of safety, and delegate to the debate on the Constitutional Convention after the war. Several of his eight children and grandchildren lived in and developed the area during the nineteenth century.

Some of the earliest settlers claimed land along Autry's (sometimes Otter's) Creek in the southern part of the county. John Stokes and Jacob Evans received land grants in the Macclesfield area as early as 1749. About that same time, William Davis Sr. purchased a Granville grant in what is now the Crisp area.

GRANVILLE DISTRICT

The general assembly found it necessary to divide the growing western and southern edges of the county into smaller counties with their own courts, so residents could more easily get to the county seat for legal and business matters. The general assembly divided Edgecombe in half in 1746 and formed Granville County, which was later divided to form Orange, Bute, and part of Warren and Vance Counties. This Granville division decreased Edgecombe County by approximately 1,750 square miles.

In 1749, the governor appointed a new group of justices that included Joseph Howell, John Haywood, Richard Whitaker, William Kinchen, Aquilla Suggs, William Taylor, John Pope, Joseph Lane, John Thomas, John Pryor, Robert Brinkley, Samuel Williams of Stoney Creek, Wallace Jones, and Edward Moore (*Colonial Records, IV*, p. 966). These men represent some of the earliest settlers in the area. A few of those names had also appeared on the 1732 Edgecombe Precinct list.

According to an article by Alan Watson in the *North Carolina Historical Review*, the early settlers lived in one or one-and-a-half room wooden houses with clapboard siding. A few lived in log cabins, while only the wealthy could afford brick homes. There were no families wealthy enough to own brick homes in what is now Edgecombe County. The dominant focus of the home was the fireplace, which was used for heating as well as cooking. Furniture was often sparse, consisting of a bed (usually just a mattress), a table, and chests. Inventories and wills indicate feather beds and table linens were found in most wealthy homes. Families had candle molds to make their own candles, and many households also had at least one spinning wheel.

As North Carolina was a royal colony, the governor authorized the establishment of a parish for the Anglican Church. According to an earlier county history by Turner and Bridgers, the earliest Episcopal church was a chapel located on the Tar River in part of Edgecombe Parish in the late 1740s. The Reverend James Moir was appointed to the parish in 1747. As the county population grew, so did that of the parish: when Granville County was separated, St. John's Parish was created. St. Mary's was formed in 1756. The vestry of St. Mary's continued to meet at the chapel on the Tar River.

Reverend Moir was one of the commissioners who organized the county seat of Tarboro, but was a controversial figure in county history. The *Colonial Records* include several reports of complaints by county residents against Moir. There are also letters to the Anglican Church from Moir complaining about the lack of

Typical farm homes were made of wood. The interior of the Silas Everette House (c. 1800) has painted wainscoting and detailed moldings showing fine craftsmanship. (Courtesy of Blount-Bridgers House Archives.)

religious participation in the local parish. Both sides made charges of misconduct and the supporting evidence makes it difficult to determine who—the minister or the residents—was telling the truth.

During the French and Indian War and the subsequent political challenges with England, the Anglican Church struggled to maintain a presence in the colonies. It almost disappeared after the American Revolution. The Great Awakening introduced other denominations throughout the south. The most successful in this area was Baptist. Prior to the Revolution, there were only four Baptist churches in the county. Kehukke Church, in what is now Halifax County, was established in 1742. Falls of the Tar River, the oldest congregation in Edgecombe County, was opened in 1757. Toisnot, now in Wilson County, was established in 1756. Fishing Creek, in the northeastern part of the county, was founded in 1777. Each church continued to grow after the Revolution.

At the outbreak of the Seven Years or French and Indian War, each colony was ordered to report its preparedness for providing troops. In 1755, a militia list in the *Colonial Records* reported that Edgecombe County had the highest number of militiamen in the colony: 1,317 out of a total male population of 2,538. Within a year, its population had increased by at least 200 men. Approximately two-thirds of the increase was accounted for by African slaves, indicating economic growth that required more labor. Although no total population figures appear for the county until the 1790 census, the estimated population in the 1750s was

Most farm homes of early settlers had sparse furnishings, including a table, chairs, and various tools, such as wheels to spin the cotton, flax, or wool into thread. Wills and inventories of eighteenth-century estates indicate that most homes had such spinning wheels.

When Tarboro was chartered in 1760, the town was laid out in 121 half-acre lots in a 5-block pattern with the Town Common on all sides of the town. This is a copy of the original plat from the 1760 deed book. (Courtesy of Edgecombe County Courthouse, Register of Deeds Office.)

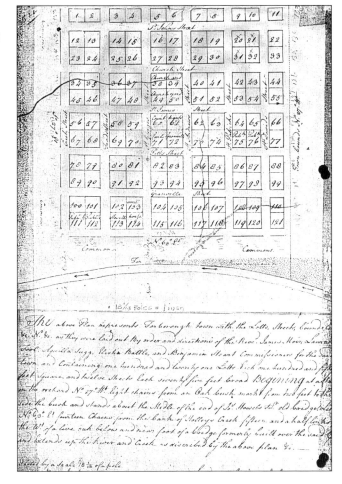

approximately 11,000. The two closest counties in population to Edgecombe were Craven (with the port town of New Bern) and Bertie, with total populations of about 7,500 each.

Even though Edgecombe had a large population, it lacked towns of significant size. The court and jail were located in Enfield, which is now a small town in Halifax County. Edenton was considered the nearest town in which to conduct major business. An unusual series of events occurred in 1758 and 1759, leading to the charter of Tarboro in 1760 and its becoming the county seat within three years. Because of its ever-increasing population, the general assembly announced plans to divide Edgecombe again in 1758. This act removed 1,200 square miles north of Fishing Creek, with the new Halifax County occupying the space between Fishing Creek and the Roanoke River. The court of Enfield was now in the new county, leaving Edgecombe without a place for conducting judicial business.

At the same time, the general assembly received another petition of complaint from the citizens of Edgecombe County regarding the questionable practices of

E 67
"ENFIELD RIOT"
———···———
Here in 1759 Lord Granville's land agents were compelled to give bond to return illegal fees. This was a fore-runner of Regulators.

ARCHIVES AND HIGHWAY DEPARTMENTS   1960

In 1759, Edgecombe citizens threatened Francis Corbin, the land agent for Lord Granville. Several were arrested and jailed in Enfield, then the county seat. Colleagues soon broke them out of jail in what is known as the Enfield Riot.

Francis Corbin, the land agent of Lord Granville. Although complaints against Corbin dated to 1755, the general assembly again did not act. Corbin was accused of selling the same property to several different clients by falsifying some points on the deeds. He also was inconsistent in the charge of fees for processing deeds and land sales.

Citizens also believed that Corbin had a local agent, John Haywood, contributing to his tainted business practices. Haywood was the local representative for Lord Granville. He moved to Edgecombe in the early 1740s and served as a justice of the peace before being elected to serve in the general assembly. By 1754, he was commander of the militia. He was also active in the Anglican Church, serving as a vestryman. Haywood died on a trip to Edenton and was brought home and buried by his family. Some residents believed that Haywood was as corrupt as Corbin and had really disappeared with their tax payments. Therefore, in December 1758, a group of men who were never identified went to the cemetery and exhumed Haywood's body to confirm its identity.

Once it was discovered that Haywood was indeed dead, the citizens confronted Corbin. Reports in the *Colonial Records* indicate that after the general assembly failed to act on the complaints at the January 1759 session, about 20 men marched to Edenton and took Corbin out of his house and threatened him unless he corrected his bad deeds and posted a table of fees. In fear for his life, Corbin agreed to whatever the men wanted. However, as soon as he returned home, he filed a complaint with Royal Governor Dobbs about his kidnapping and harsh treatment. This time Governor Dobbs did respond, by arresting several men in Edgecombe County and placing them in the Enfield jail in Halifax County. In return, another group of men attacked the jail, freed those inside, and destroyed the building in the process. Corbin refused to pursue the charges, either because he was warned not to or because he realized that a trial would expose his corrupt business. No one was ever charged with breaking into and destroying the jail, because—as concluded in the *Colonial Records*—it would have been difficult for the justices to bring charges against themselves. This ended what was known as the Enfield Riots. In a report to London, Governor Dobbs wrote "these mobs, riots, and insurrections terrible as they are were all confined to Lord Granville's northern district and all the outrages complained of were limited to the counties of Granville and Edgecombe."

TARBORO CHARTERED

Amongst all the turmoil, Edgecombe citizens needed a courthouse. From 1759 to 1763, court convened at Redmond's Old Field. Meanwhile, landowner Joseph Howell deeded over 150 acres of land along the Tar River to establish a town. Five

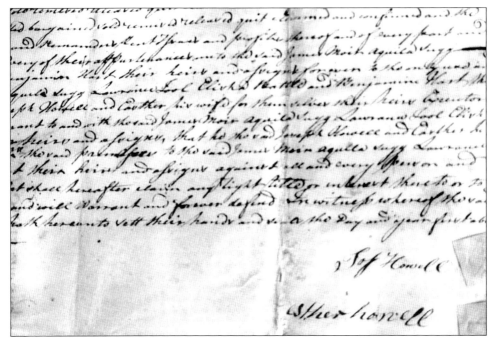

Joseph Howell and his wife Esther sold to five commissioners 150 acres of land that became Tarboro. This was the original charter for the town.

men—Reverend James Moir, Aquilla Suggs, Lawrence Toole, Elisha Battle, and Benjamin Hart—were selected as town commissioners and given the task of laying out the town. They planned a town with 121 half-acre lots in a grid system with streets 70 feet wide. They set aside 50 acres surrounding the town as a common that also marked the town's borders. On November 30, 1760, the general assembly approved the town and named it Tarborough.

The new town occupied land on the northwest side of a bend of the Tar River consisting of six blocks with the common fronting the river on the south, Joshua Street (now Wilson Street) on the north, what is now Panola Street on the east, and Creek Street (now Albemarle Avenue) on the west. The commissioners created eight public lots, four near the river. Lots 72 and 73 in the center of town were to be used for a courthouse and jail. Lots 74 and 75 were set aside for a public cemetery.

The original streets were named for location, political figures, and religious saints. The east-west street near the river was named for Lord Granville. The next was named Pitt Street in honor of William Pitt, prime minister of England, followed by St. James Street, Church Street, St. John Street, and St. Joshua Street.

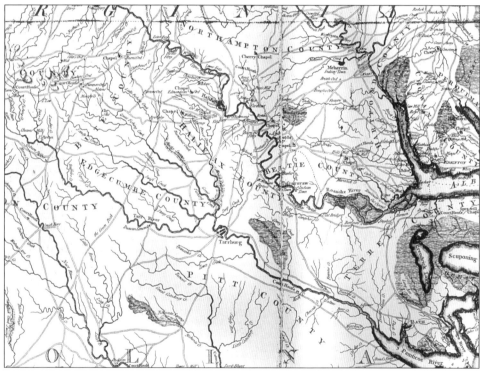

The Mouzon Map of 1775 shows the county seat of Tarrburg in the bend of the Tarr River with various roads leading to other North Carolina communities. It also shows the various tributaries where early settlers chose to live such as Town Creek, Stony Creek, and Fishing Creek. (Courtesy of North Carolina Office of Archives and History.)

The north-south streets were Creek Street; Trade Street, where businesses were to build; St. George Street, for the patron saint of England (now Main Street); St. Andrew Street, for the patron saint of Scotland; St. Patrick Street, for the patron saint of Ireland; and St. David Street, for the patron saint of Wales.

Tarborough (also presented on maps as Tarrburg) was a river port. It is the most inland point of navigation on the Tar River and also the crossroads of two main highways through the northeastern corner of the colony. The town grew as a trading center with warehouses along the river. Naval stores (tar and turpentine), pork, and corn were the most important exports until tobacco appeared in 1770s. Citizens also imported goods from England. Other crops such as corn, wheat, and sweet potatoes were also produced—although mainly for local use and not export. Cattle and hogs were the primary livestock. Fruit trees were naturally abundant and peach brandy was a popular by-product.

Most of the lots were sold and the town of Tarborough began to grow, although not fast enough. In 1772, Henry Irwin was elected to represent Tarboro in the general assembly, but the town did not yet have the 60 families required for representation. Little is known about Irwin's early life. He apparently moved to Edgecombe County from Virginia. Although he could not represent Tarboro in 1772, he was appointed to represent the county at the Provincial Congress at Halifax in 1776. This body passed the Halifax Resolves, which provided North Carolina with representatives at the Continental Congress in Philadelphia to vote for independence.

THE AMERICAN REVOLUTION

There are no records to indicate if any local men served in the French and Indian or Seven Years War, even though the local militia was activated. Because of mistrust of the royal government, Edgecombe acquired a reputation for not assisting authorities. During the Regulator movement in the early 1770s, in which citizens of several backcountry counties protested unfair taxes (and which some believe had its origins in the Enfield Riots of 1758–1759), Governor William Tryon requested militia troops to help put down an insurrection in Alamance and Orange Counties. Edgecombe refused.

During the unrest with the British after the Seven Years War, Edgecombe citizens did participate in several activities that lead to the American Revolution. During the Stamp Act crisis, a local group of the Sons of Liberty formed in 1765. Colonel Haywood reported in April 1765 that Edgecombe had a militia of 14 companies with 1,317 men. Despite this raising of troops, Edgecombe failed to send delegates to the first Revolutionary Congress.

On the eve of the American Revolution, Edgecombe County had a scattered population of approximately 4,000 citizens including 1,000 slaves. Most of Edgecombe supported the patriot cause. Elisha Battle headed the Committee of Safety in 1774, and in 1775 he, along with Haywood, Duncan Lemon, Henry Irwin, and Nathanial Boddie, attended the Provincial Congress in Hillsborough.

The plaque in the Edgecombe County Courthouse was dedicated in 1919 by the North Carolina Historical Commission. It recognizes Colonel Jonas Johnston, who died in 1779 fighting in the Revolutionary War on the side of the Patriots.

Jonas Johnston gave an inspirational speech in Tarborough and raised volunteers, then led a company of militiamen at Moore's Creek in February 1776. After the battle, he went to the convention in Halifax to form the state constitution. In 1779, Johnston commanded a militia unit in South Carolina under Richard Caswell. Johnston fought at Stono Ferry in South Carolina where he "greatly distinguished himself for his personal courage." He was reassigned to the Upper Pee Dee to join Greene's troops and died from illness along the way. He was buried in a friend's family plot near the South Carolina/North Carolina border. His wife, Esther Maund Johnston, survived until 1840 and is buried at a cemetery near Vinedale near Pinetops. The county has placed a plaque in the Edgecombe County Courthouse to commemorate Johnston.

Another Edgecombe citizen to die in the war was Henry Irwin. Irwin was appointed lieutenant colonel of the 5th regiment of the North Carolina Continental Line. He led a group of Continentals to put down a loyalist uprising, known as the Llewyllen Conspiracy. Afterwards, he served with the Continental Army and was killed in the Battle of Germantown.

Elisha Battle represented the county at the Provincial Congress in Halifax in April 1776. Other county residents volunteered to serve in the local militia and some served in Washington's Continental Army. In the midst of the conflict, Edgecombe County was divided again and Nash County was formed in 1777. The boundary was at John Powell's on Fishing Creek, running to the Falls of the Tar and then to Contentnea. Everything east of this line remained Edgecombe County, while everything west became Nash County (named in honor of General Francis Nash, who died in the American Revolution at Germantown). Its county seat was Nash Court House until 1815, when Nashville was established. Approximately 400 men from Nash and Edgecombe Counties served in the Revolutionary War.

There were no battles in the county, but Cornwallis and his men were engaged by snipers along Fishing Creek as they crossed into Halifax County on the way to Yorktown. Henry Irwin Toole was among the first to accept a commission in the Continental Army and fought at Brandywine. He returned to Tarboro after the

The Miles Harvey Chapter of the Daughters of the American Revolution and the North Carolina Historical Commission dedicated this plaque in 1920. It remembers Lieutenant Colonel Henry Irwin, who was killed in the battle of Germantown on October 4, 1777. The plaque was moved to the current courthouse when it opened in 1964.

war and resumed life as a merchant. Ned Griffin, a former slave, was given his freedom for fighting in the war. The act that freed Griffin stated that he:

> should faithfully serve as a soldier in the continental line of this state for and during the term of twelve months; and whereas the said Ned Griffin did faithfully on his part perform the condition . . . that the said Ned Griffin, later the property of William Kitchen, shall forever hereafter be in every respect declared a freeman; and he shall be, and he is hereby enfranchised and forever delivered and discharged from the yoke of slavery.

Host to the North Carolina General Assembly in 1785 and 1787, Tarboro was one of several towns where the legislature met, as no permanent state capital had been declared. During its stay from November 19 to December 22, 1787, the assembly passed 56 bills and argued the proposed United States Constitution.

Edgecombe County sent Elisha Battle, Blythel Bell, Robert Diggs, William Fort, and Etherlred Gray to the State Ratification Convention in July–August

Thomas Blount (1759–1812) served in Congress representing this area until his death. (Courtesy of North Carolina Office of Archives and History.)

1788, to debate the proposed United States Constitution. These men were anti-Federalists who opposed the Constitution and supported the Articles of Confederation, which gave states more freedom. They insisted on a bill of rights to protect individuals. The anti-Federalists were the majority at this convention and voted 184–33 against the Constitution.

Another convention was held in Fayetteville in November 1789 and new delegates were sent. Thomas Blount, Jeremiah Hilliard, and Ethelred Philips—all Federalists—joined William Fort and Ethelred Gray. Gray died during the convention and did not vote; apparently Fort was convinced to support the Federalists.

Between 1777 and 1790, North Carolina debated the location of a new capital. Seven towns—including Tarboro, Fayetteville, and Hillsborough—joined in the bidding. Tarboro came within three votes, but no town received enough votes for a majority. Eventually, Wake County was selected and Raleigh was created as the capital city.

The 1790s were busy years for Edgecombe County. The population was over 10,000—including 70 free blacks and over 3,000 slaves. A new courthouse was completed in 1790. President George Washington visited Tarboro in April 1791, and stayed in a tavern on St. George Street, after receiving a one-gun salute—as the militia only had one artillery piece. Jacob Battle, Edward Hall, and Amos Johnson, among others, demonstrated an interest in education by raising money to charter an academy in 1793, although it was not active for several more years. Thomas Blount was elected to the United States Congress in 1792 and served until 1798.

April 1798 was noted for severe weather. A tornado damaged homes and felled trees throughout Tarboro. Supreme Court Justice James Iredell was traveling to court when he was stranded in Tarboro by a flood that washed away the bridge over the Tar River. In a letter to his wife, he indicated that all the bridges in the area had been damaged, but one was repaired near Colonel Mayo's home. There, Iredell learned most of the bridges in the Coneta (Conetoe) area were also gone. With the help of some slaves from the Pippen farm, a bridge was repaired that enabled Iredell to get to Williamston in Martin County, although he was unable to get through to Savannah. Iredell was told that the river was higher than it been in over 20 years.

In the last year of the decade, Thomas Blount went to the North Carolina Senate and Elisha Battle—who had been active in the county for 50 years—died, but left several sons to carry on his tradition of economic and political activity in the county.

2. THE ANTEBELLUM YEARS OF GROWTH AND PROSPERITY 1800–1860

The nineteenth century continued growth and prosperity in the area. Although Tarboro did not become the state capital, Edgecombe County continued to thrive. In 1800, only 200 more people were in the county than in the decade before. By 1810, the county population increased from 10,421 to 12,423. Another 1,000 were added by 1820. The rate of growth continued by about 1,000 per decade until 1850, when the population reached over 17,000. Approximately half of the population were slaves, as the county became one of the leading cotton-producing counties in the state. Tarboro, which had a population of just over 500 in 1800, doubled to over 1,000 by 1850. The river ports of Tarboro and Sparta (later changed by the United States Postal Service to Old Sparta) had warehouses for storing goods being shipped down river.

Thomas Blount (1759–1812) became a leading political figure and landowner after the Revolution. His brother William Blount was the territorial governor of Tennessee, signed the United States Constitution, and later was censured in Congress for land deals in Tennessee. Another brother, John Gray Blount, ran the family shipping business and helped establish the town of Washington, North Carolina. Three of the Blount brothers were among the largest landowners in the new United States, owning land from the Atlantic Ocean to the Mississippi River and operating wharves, warehouses, ships, saw mills, gristmills, tanneries, and cotton gins, as well as owning numerous slaves.

Thomas managed the Tarboro branch of the business, running shipping and mercantile operations. He served under General Jethro Sumner of Warren County during the American Revolution and was captured and taken to England as a prisoner of war. After the war, Blount served as a trustee of the University of North Carolina and a commissioner of the town of Raleigh, and was elected to Congress from 1804–1812. Blount died in Washington, D.C. while Congress was in session in April 1812. He was buried in the Congressional Cemetery there.

Mary "Jackie" Sumner Blount (1777–1822) was the wife of Congressman Blount and the daughter of General Jethro Sumner. She was one of the wealthiest women in Tarboro in the early 1800s. (Courtesy of Blount-Bridgers House Archives.)

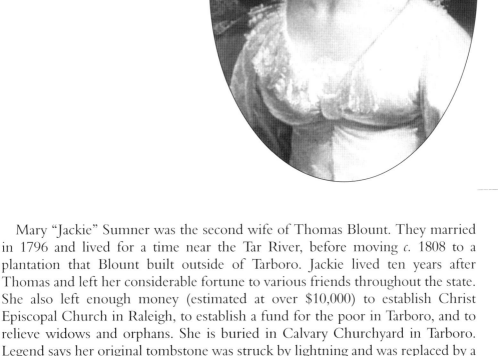

Mary "Jackie" Sumner was the second wife of Thomas Blount. They married in 1796 and lived for a time near the Tar River, before moving *c.* 1808 to a plantation that Blount built outside of Tarboro. Jackie lived ten years after Thomas and left her considerable fortune to various friends throughout the state. She also left enough money (estimated at over $10,000) to establish Christ Episcopal Church in Raleigh, to establish a fund for the poor in Tarboro, and to relieve widows and orphans. She is buried in Calvary Churchyard in Tarboro. Legend says her original tombstone was struck by lightning and was replaced by a gift from the women of Christ Church.

Theophilus Parker was a friend and business associate of Thomas Blount, and president of the Bank of Tarboro. In 1810, Parker built a fine two-story home on Church Street. He was a merchant who also owned a sizable plantation. He was part owner of the ship *Snap Dragon*, captained by Otway Burns. The *Snap Dragon* was a successful privateer in the War of 1812, capturing numerous prizes worth about half a million dollars before being captured herself in 1814. Research by Hugh Buckner on "Muster Rolls of the Soldiers of the War of 1812: Detached from the Militia of North Carolina in 1812 & 1814" reveals that over 300 soldiers from Edgecombe County served in the War of 1812. Members from the North Carolina 1st and 2nd Regiments also were sent to the U.S. Army in 1814.

Jeremiah Battle was a grandson of Elisha Battle, the aforementioned land owner and commissioner of Tarboro. He attended the University of North Carolina and was active in numerous political, economic, and social aspects of the county. He was one of the area's doctors before moving to Raleigh in the 1820s. In 1811, he delivered a report to the Agricultural Society of Edgecombe County, of which he was secretary, on the history and status of the area. Battle described the natural flora and fauna, the many creeks and bridges, and the agricultural use of the land, along with a brief history of the county and some of its prominent citizens. He discussed everything from politics and history to limited education. He listed over 30 types of businesses in the county including stores, a blacksmith, a carriage shop, shoemakers, wheelwrights, and cabinet makers. He described the town in 1810:

> Tarborough is the only town in the county. It is handsomely situated on the sw bank of Tar river. . . . The streets are 72 feet wide and cross each other at right angles leaving squares of two acres each. These squares being divided into half acre lots, makes every lot front two streets. There are about 50 private houses in it, and generally from 15–20 stores; a church, gaol [jail], tobacco warehouse and a large court house which was used for the sitting of the State Legislature.

The Grove, built c. 1808, was the home of Thomas Blount—soldier, statesman, and merchant—who was one of the largest land owners. This exceptional Federal-style home was set on a large plantation just north of Tarboro.

Battle went on to point out that only the jail and one store were brick with all other structures in town being wooden, but "a few were well built private homes" that were "generally plain and cheap." Battle credited the finest home in the county to Thomas Blount. He described the livestock as primarily hogs, along with some cattle, sheep, and mules (which had replaced horses as work animals). He then identified the local industries:

> The "Manufactories" are only such as serve our domestic purposes, & consist of the following . . . Looms 933 in number; in which are woven annually about 150,000 yards of different kinds of cloth. . . . 159 Distilleries, in which are annually distilled 39,000 Gallons of peach & apple brandy. . . . 439 Tanneries, in which are tanned annually 1,964 Hides. . . . Mechanics—31 Black-smith shops, 4 Hatters shops, 2 Cabinet shops, 6 Saddlers shops. . . . 3 Carriage shops . . . 3 Shoemakers' shops . . . [and] others . . . such as Turners, Coopers, Wheelwrights, &c. . . . There are 29 cotton machines, working 509 Saws.

In a chart, Dr. Battle listed the produce of 21 stores or farms in the county (14 in Tarboro), which exported:

> over 6,325 barrels of corn; 6,850 bushels of peas; 2,042 barrels pork; 8,210 lbs of tallow; 8,170 lbs beeswax; 43,240 lbs of cotton; 1,262 bushel of flaxseed; 9,413 barrels of naval stores; 124,300 lbs bacon; 556 kegs of lard; 243 heads of tobacco; 145 barrels of brandy; 73 barrels of flour; 2740 bushels wheat; 150 fur skins; 158 bushels of beans; 70 bushels of oats; and 3,000 lbs beef.

All of these products were shipped down river on flat bottom boats, or later steamboats, to coastal ports and then on to larger cities. While all of this was for export, Battle indicated that "the town is generally well supplied from the county with fresh beef, lambs, pigs, poultry, eggs, butter, honey, fruit, melons."

EDUCATION AND BUILDING SCHOOLS

In 1811, Jeremiah Battle reported, "there are 17 schools in the county . . . not teaching more than reading, writing, and arithmetic. . . .[W]e may discover that is progressing . . . for 50 years ago there was not more than one or two schools in the limits of the whole county." Battle's report possibly inspired others to consider the importance of education in the county. Between 1812 and 1820, Exum Lewis established a school on his plantation, Mount Prospect, west of Leggett, and brought in teachers from Virginia, Florida, and Ireland.

In 1813, efforts began to establish a school, which was constructed in 1814 on an acre of the town common at the banks of Hendricks Creek. The trustees for this Academy of Tarborough were Jeremiah Battle, F.L. Dancy, E.D. McNair,

Mount Prospect, the home of Exum Lewis, was constructed in the Leggett area in the second half of the eighteenth century and served as stagecoach stop in the early nineteenth century. Lewis also operated an academy on his plantation in the 1820s. The house caught fire in the 1970s and was eventually demolished. (Courtesy of North Carolina Office of Archives and History.)

Robert Joyner, Bennet Barrow, James West Clark, Joel Battle, James Southerland, H.A. Donaldson, Peter Evans, and Carey Whitaker. The school opened in 1815 with Robert Hall as headmaster. Tuition ranged between $16 and $22, depending on languages and mathematic courses taken. Several teachers, both male and female, worked at the academy for the first few years. By 1823, females were admitted as the school differentiated male and female departments. (In 1840, those departments were separated into Male and Female Academies.) Miss Anna Ragsdale instructed at the female school from its inception for over 19 years. Mr. Eugene Farnan, originally from Ireland, took over the male department in 1824. Each year, the Tarborough Academy averaged 70 students from several surrounding counties.

In the 1820s, several other private schools were created including Sparta Academy, New Hope Academy, Columbia Academy, Cedar Hill, Hopewell Academy, Friendship Academy, Hickory Grove, Toisnot, and Conetoe. An 1835 ad in the *Tarborough Press* announced that Conetoe school students could board "in the neighborhood for 10 cents a day or from $3.50 per month." In the 1830s, Mark Bennett opened Town Creek Academy. Several smaller private schools also opened, while public schools were not approved by county voters until the late 1830s.

The Tarborough Academy reported upcoming "Academy Exams" in the June 4, 1830 *Free Press*. Parents of students and interested community citizens witnessed the semi-annual examinations whereby students presented musical programs and speeches and completed oral exams. According to the reporter,

> The flourishing state of the Academy, comprising upwards of fifty young ladies, is a source of much pride and gratification to our citizens. The scene closed with an Examination of the Senior Class, consisting of Laura P. Clark, Dehla Dancy, Mary R. Hearn, Mary W. Pugh, and Emily Mathewson. These young ladies having passed through all the studies of the Academy and sustained a critical examination of them, were permitted to graduate with the warmest approbation of the Trustees.

One student at the Academy was Laura Clark, the daughter of James West Clark and his wife Arabella Toole Clark. She married John W. Cotton two years after her graduation. Her brother Henry Toole Clark became governor of the state during the Civil War. Another student was Eugenia Bell, daughter of Fredrick Bell and

Piney Prospect, the 1790s home of Peter Evans, is located near Old Sparta. The house is somewhat unusual with a side chimney and closed ends of the double porch. Evans was one of the trustees of the Tarborough Academy. (Courtesy of Library of Congress; print at Blount-Bridgers House Archives.)

his wife Elizabeth, who was 15 when she attended the academy. In October 1832, she wrote a letter to her friend Eleanor Page, who lived near Scotland Neck in Halifax County. Eugenia revealed that she was very busy with her lessons:

> I have to study very hard indeed to get my lesson. I have to get two pages in Rhetorick, 4 in Philosophy, 2 chapters in History, 2 pages in Geography and one in the back part of Arithmetic which is very hard.

Eugenia invited Eleanor to the examinations that took place in June 1833 and included five graduates: Elizabeth Joyner, Martha Clark, Mary Sumner Clark, Esther Bond, and Martha Bond. Mary Sumner Clark was the goddaughter of Mrs. Thomas Blount and the sister of Laura Clark, who had graduated in 1830. Eugenia probably graduated in 1834, as her wedding announcement appeared in the April 1835 paper. She married William McGee of Shelby County, Tennessee and moved to his home.

Female students soon outnumbered males at the academy, so a separate building was constructed around 1840, when the departments separated formally into the Male and Female Tarboro Academies. Female students remained in the original building on Hendricks Creek, while males enjoyed a new structure built

Local merchant Spencer Cotton built this house on east Church Street in the 1820s. During the 1850s, Reverend Owen and his wife operated a private school in this home. The structure was renovated in the 1860s and featured interior frescoes by E.V. Zoeller. In 1868, George Howard purchased the property.

at the opposite end of the common facing west on St. Patrick Street. Young men occupied that site until the Civil War, when the students exchanged buildings. Numerous ads in the local paper advertised the classes with tuition averaging $12 to $15 a session, depending on the course load. In 1841, the ads indicated that students could board with local families for $6 to $8 a month.

In 1846, Reverend Thomas R. Owen and his wife became teachers at the Female Academy, where they continued until 1852. The announcement signed by the trustees stated that Mr. Owen had graduated from the University of North Carolina and his wife had completed school in Philadelphia. Tuition was $10 a session, $20 for music with the use of the piano. In 1852, the Owens opened their own private school. A former student, Joseph Blount Cheshire—who later became Bishop of North Carolina—recalled fond memories of these teachers. In a manuscript, "Some Account of My Life for My Children," he described the Owens:

> They were, both of them, quite superior in talents and in social and intellectual culture, though very different in individual character and temperament. . . . [Mr. Owen] was a Presbyterian minister when I first remember him, while Mrs. Owen was an intense Baptist. There were no Presbyterians in Tarboro and I have understood that his Baptist wife made it impracticable for him to be the acceptable pastor of a Presbyterian Church. In his theology, he was a hard and dry Calvinist, entirely in sympathy with the prevailing Baptist sentiment.
>
> He was a scholar and a man of keen and cultivated intellect, quite capable, and doubtless those of his pupils, who desired to learn and who studied diligently, gained something from him. He liked to converse with intelligent and well-informed people. . . .
>
> Mrs. Owen, on the contrary, was a born teacher, loved the work, and felt its high dignity and privilege. She was a strict disciplinarian, but just and generous, and appreciative of good qualities in others. She had a simple dignity and grace which would have made her a person of distinction in any company. I believe all her pupils admired and loved her, though they stood in some awe of her.

When the Owens left, Miss Angelia Crandell, a graduate of the Troy Female Seminary in New York, became the new teacher. Meanwhile, the Male Academy underwent several different changes in principals. Mr. Robert Lindsay was hired in 1848. After two years, he moved to Alabama to practice law and was elected governor of Alabama in 1870. Other principals included Robert Winborne from 1850–1852, H.B. Farrar from 1852–1858, and Frank Wilkinson from 1858 until the school burned in 1885.

The Hendricks Creek building was destroyed by fire in 1885. The Female Academy also suffered a major fire in the 1891. It was renovated and continued operation until 1909, when the school board purchased the property to build Bridgers School.

William Smith Battle (1823–1915) was one of the wealthiest land owners in Edgecombe County prior to the Civil War. He owned Rocky Mount Mills and thousands of acres, according to the 1860 census. This portrait is in the Blount-Bridgers House.

ROCKY MOUNT MILLS AND THE BATTLE FAMILY

In 1818, Joel Battle, Peter Evans, and Henry Donaldson established a small textile mill at the Falls of the Tar River. This was the second such mill in the state and grew to include a grist mill, as well as the cotton mill. It soon became the center of a new community named Rocky Mount for the rocks along the river. The mill was first operated by slaves, then by women. Joel Battle bought out his partners and in the 1830s Joel's cousin James Smith Battle purchased the mill. He, and then his son William Smith Battle, operated the mill for the next 40 years.

James Battle, another grandson of Elisha Battle, inherited the family plantation, Cool Spring, with 20,000 acres and several hundred slaves. Battle was involved in a landmark case of the North Carolina Supreme Court. In *State v. Will, Slave of James S. Battle*, 1834, Battle became the first slave owner in the South to have his slave defended against the charge of killing a white man. Following tradition of the time, the lower court automatically found Will guilty of murder in the death of his overseer, Richard Baxter. Battle appealed the case to the state supreme court, which ruled:

> Judgment upon the special verdict, that the prisoner is not guilty of the
> murder, wherewith he stands charged but is guilty of the felonious

slaying and killing Richard Baxter. . . . If a slave, in defence [sic] of his life, and under circumstances strongly calculated to excite his passions of terror and resentment, kills his overseer, the homicide is, by such circumstances, mitigated to manslaughter.

In addition to working in the mill and on the various Battle plantations, his slaves built part of the Wilmington and Weldon Railroad. The W&W Railroad was completed in 1840, and at that time was the longest in the country. It was part of the Whigs' progressive plan for the state, which included expanding transportation routes. The railroad was originally to be built from Raleigh to Wilmington, but due to changes in support and finances, it changed route north

William F. Dancy married Mary Eliza Battle in January 1858 at her home, Cool Spring. Mary was the daughter of James Smith Battle, one of the largest plantation owners in the county. She was the great-granddaughter of Elisha Battle, one of the first town commissioners. (Portrait courtesy of North Carolina Museum of History in Raleigh.)

of Goldsboro to go north to Weldon and connect to the Virginia state line. James Battle stepped in and provided not only financial support, but also the labor to build much of the railroad through from what is now Wilson County north to Halifax County. A supply area set up for the railroad crews between Rocky Mount and the Halifax County line evolved into the community of Battleboro.

Later, this railroad became the county line between Nash and Edgecombe Counties. The railroad served to improve transportation of farm products and to connect Edgecombe with other trade centers. Eventually, ties were formed with Richmond and Raleigh as additional lines were added. In 1860, a spur line ran from Rocky Mount to Tarboro.

POLITICAL DEVELOPMENT

Edgecombe County continued to elect representatives to state and sometimes national offices. After the death of Thomas Blount, his seat in Congress was held by James West Clark and then by Dr. Thomas Hall. Clark served one term in

Dr. William Sparkman Baker (1810–1861) was a physician and plantation owner. He served in the state general assembly from 1838 to 1841. He was the first of three generations of Bakers to become doctors in Edgecombe County. (Courtesy of North Carolina Office of Archives and History.)

Congress, but before and after that he served in the North Carolina General Assembly and the North Carolina Senate. During the Jackson administration, he was chief clerk of the U.S. Navy Department. He encouraged his son, Henry Toole Clark, to enter politics.

Hall lost his congressional seat after the controversial presidential election of 1824, in which Congress decided the outcome. Hall supported Crawford rather than Jackson for president. When Hall ran for congress again in 1825, he was challenged and bested by Richard Hines. Hall reclaimed his seat in 1827, and managed to keep it despite a strong campaign waged by Joseph Ross Lloyd. In all, Hall served eight terms in Congress representing the conservatives in the region. He was finally defeated by a Whig candidate in 1835, and returned to North Carolina to serve in the state senate. After that term ended, Hall retired to his plantation in Edgecombe County to practice medicine.

During the 1830s and 1840s, county residents had elaborate July Fourth programs. The newspaper would often dedicate over a half page to coverage, listing dozens of speakers and the many cheers and tributes given to the country. Francis Bond sponsored a "Grand Exhibition of Fire Works" on Monday, July 5, 1847. (The celebration was postponed a day because the Fourth was on a Sunday.) The amazing pyrotechnic exhibition featured a hot air balloon.

Born in Edgecombe County in 1789, Louis Dicken Wilson represented Edgecombe County in the North Carolina General Assembly from 1814 to 1846. He served as a delegate to the 1835 state constitutional convention and was an advocate of public schools. Wilson, a Democrat, survived several challenges by Whigs, who in the 1830s gained control of many of the state offices. Trained in law, he was also the tax collector for Tarboro. He purchased the Grove, the former home of Thomas and "Jackie" Blount. Wilson resigned his seat in the general assembly to serve in the Mexican War.

In the election of 1848, Whig candidate and Mexican War hero Zachary Taylor ran against moderate Democrat Lewis Cass. Although Taylor carried the state, Cass was the choice of a majority of the voting residents of Edgecombe County, with 1,326 votes to Taylor's 142. Both the county and the state had supported James K. Polk in 1844.

THE PRESS AND BUSINESSES

In 1826, George Howard, a printer from Maryland, relocated to Tarboro from Halifax County, where he had been producing *The Free Press*. He brought the paper with him and continued publishing it, weekly on Fridays, for another ten years. Subscribers paid $2 per year in advance or 25¢ per month.

By 1836, Howard changed the name of his newspaper to *The Tarborough Press*. In addition to local news, weather, and political events from the state and the nation, the paper featured local advertisements. Often the ads announced sales at dry good stores, carriage makers, and cabinet makers. James Weddell sold dry goods. A.C. Howard sold ladies dresses. D. Richards and Company operated a

"Cheap Store." John Wilson made and repaired cotton gins. Coffield King sold gentlemen's clothing. N.H. Rountree sold hardware, cutlery, and crockery. In January 1831, G.B. King announced a dancing school would open in February. Occasionally some ads announced the sale of plantations, as their owners moved west. There were also notices of runaway slaves.

The August 20, 1830 *Tarborough Press* presented the local totals of the 1830 federal census completed by assistant marshal Isaac Norfleet. The official report revealed that there were a total of 565 residents in Tarboro:

Free white persons	133 males and 131 females
Slaves	113 males and 173 females
Free colored persons	7 males and 8 females

The population for the county was almost 15,000 persons—7,630 whites, 7,075 slaves, and 238 free colored people—indicating that the area was still predominately rural. The marshal's report on Tarboro continued:

> [The town] contains at present a courthouse and jail, 2 meeting houses, a branch of the state bank, post office, printing office and female academy, 10 stores and 3 taverns, 4 doctors and 3 lawyers, 3 tailor shops, 2 milliners', 2 saddlers, 2 shoemakers', 1 coachmaker, 1 cabinet maker, 1 machinist, and 1 barbershop. . . . Although the town has increase in population its trade has decreased considerably having formerly contained 23 stores.

The cabinet maker listed in the 1830 census was Lewis Bond, who had moved to Tarboro from Pitt County around 1820. He employed one man to help him create furniture such as sideboards, desks, and bureaus. Bond expanded his business and by the 1830s, included several apprentices. An announcement in the September 15, 1846 newspaper indicated that Lewis Bond was retiring and his son Francis would now manage the firm located on Main Street. The business had grown so much that it now produced all types of furniture from sideboards and bureaus, to secretaries, dining tables, bedsteads, and all styles of sofas and chairs. Francis Lewis Bond continued the business for another 40 years. Meanwhile, Francis's wife Martha maintained a dressmaking shop in Tarboro and even advertised that she had made clothes for Queen Victoria. Emily Bond, daughter of Lewis Bond and his first wife Siddy Nelson, married Irish immigrant James Mehegan, who was a tailor. For many years, he operated a tailor shop in town and also worked with his brother-in-law.

Lancelot Johnson was another interesting businessman in this time period. In 1833, he invented a cotton oil machine and began the first cotton seed oil company in Tarboro.

In 1835, Edgecombe County replaced its old courthouse—which had been in use since the 1760s—with a brick structure on the corner of Main and St. James Streets. That courthouse served the county for over 125 years with a remodeling in 1911.

Mary Lloyd Gregory began with a boarding house in Tarboro in 1795 and built it into a fine hotel, which she managed until her death in the 1850s. She had one child, Joseph Ross Lloyd, who graduated from the University of North Carolina and became a successful businessman and president of the local branch of the state bank.

MARY LLOYD GREGORY

Mary Lloyd was 13 years old in 1781, when her father died and his will apprenticed her to the Sessoms family. She had no money or inheritance. Sometime in the 1790s, she met a young merchant named Joseph Ross and in June of 1796, they had a child, Joseph Ross Lloyd. Ross left Tarboro—first for Petersburg, then settling in Raleigh—but not before deeding Mary a small house on Church Street. Mary raised her young son and supported him by using her home as a boarding house.

In 1807, Mary attracted the attention of Edmund Gregory and they married. North Carolina property laws at that time gave husbands control of a wife's property, so Mary transferred the title of her home to her young son. Shortly after the marriage, Gregory left for Tennessee and in 1814, Mary filed petitions for

Joseph Ross purchased this home for Mary Lloyd in 1796. Originally located on Church Street, Mary operated it as a boarding house. This structure was owned by the Lawrence and Lichenstein families before being relocated to Philips Street. It is one of the oldest existing houses in Tarboro.

divorce by desertion. Although Mary eventually won her case, Gregory's protests were long and unpleasant. Finally in 1836, all claims by Gregory and his children by a previous marriage were resolved.

Meanwhile, young Joseph Lloyd attended the University of North Carolina courtesy of his father. Lloyd graduated in 1815 and studied law, probably with George Mordecai. Lloyd returned to Tarboro and was elected to the state legislature in 1821. He worked as an attorney, as postmaster of Tarboro, and president of the Tarboro branch of the North Carolina Bank. He married Maria Pugh of Bertie County and the couple had a daughter, Mary, and four sons, Henry, George Mordecai, Whitmel, and Joseph Jr.

Mary continued her boarding house business and by the 1830s, owned several lots in Tarboro. Her tavern was located on Main Street with a stable behind it. Newspapers referred to it as the "Tarboro Hotel" and later as "Mrs. Gregory's Hotel." She also purchased land outside town on Conetoe Creek and built a mill. Mary was listed as one of the charter members of Calvary Episcopal Church in 1833.

Joseph Ross Lloyd died in 1841, leaving the bulk of his estate to his children and his mother. Mary continued to invest her assets. By 1850, she owned at least six lots in town, including several warehouses along the river. Her hotel took up half of the 400 block of Main Street. The 1850 census stated she had $25,000 worth of real estate and another $26,000 of farm land with additional assets, making her the wealthiest woman in Tarboro.

Mary Lloyd Gregory died on August 7, 1858 at the age of 90. She was buried in Calvary with an elaborate monument. In his recollections of Tarboro, Bishop Cheshire described her as "a picturesque character, a woman of strength and intelligence, and among the best known and most forceful of the inhabitants of Tarboro in the days of his youth." Her obituary was published in the *Tarboro Southerner* on August 7, 1858:

> In this place, on Thursday morning the 5th inst., Mrs. Mary Gregory in the 90th year of her age. In her were united to a remarkable degree strength of mind and vigor of constitution. Left at an early age to the guidance of her own footsteps in life she has shown uncommon capacity in the management of her private affairs and leaves behind her a name and reputation that will long be held in affectionate remembrance by her relatives and friends. For more than half a century she has been known as the Proprietress of a popular Hotel in this village. It can emphatically be said of her that she was the architect of her own fortune. Commencing life without a penny, she has by her own unaided energy, foresight, and perseverance, accumulated a large property, the largest we believe ever accumulated by a woman in this county.
>
> She died quietly, peacefully and without any fears for the future. For weeks past her vigorous frame has been gradually yielding to the slow but sure work of time. She went down without disease, like an expiring taper, which had exhausted itself. Of a strong and decided character, she was warm in her friendships and kind almost to a fault with her servants. For many years she had survived her only child—a son—and leaves behind her to mourn her loss, four grandchildren, three sons and a daughter, children of the late Joseph R. Lloyd. Of no disease of no distemper died / But fell like autumn fruit that ripened long.

Mary Gregory left her estate to her four surviving grandchildren. George had died in 1856 and is buried in Calvary next to his father. Henry, the eldest, died in 1860 of pneumonia. Mary married a Caldwell. Whitmel married Harriet Howard and they had three children before Harriet died in 1861. Whitmel was a member of the Edgecombe Guards and became the company captain after John. L. Bridgers retired. Whitmel then married Laura Pender, and is buried with his wife in the J.J. Pender family plot also in Calvary Churchyard. Perhaps ironically, the richest woman in Edgecombe County signed her will with an X because she could not write her name.

MEXICAN WAR AND DEATH OF WILSON

Louis Wilson of Edgecombe County was elected to the North Carolina Senate in 1846, after having served several terms in the legislature. Wilson voted in support of the Mexican War, but a young man challenged him on behalf of the young men who would do the fighting. Wilson, who was 55 at this time, resigned his senate seat. After his farewell address, numerous resolutions were adopted complimenting his service to the state. Wilson returned to Edgecombe County on January 2, 1847, and raised a regiment to join the army in Mexico. Wilson was elected captain of the company with over 150 men, and all boarded the train to Wilmington. By the end of the month, another hundred men volunteered. They left for the war in February 1847, as Company A under command of Wilson and Company E under Captain William Duggan. Forty-seven of the men died in Mexico.

The ladies of the county "with commendable patriotism had prepared an appropriate Banner for the Volunteers. . . . Miss Sarah E. Howard on behalf of the Ladies delivered the Address to Capt. Wilson" (*Tarboro Press*, January 23, 1847). He was promoted to colonel upon arrival in Mexico. After a march to Mexico City, Wilson came down with a fever and died in August 1847 in Mexico. His body remained there until the war ended in 1848 and then was sent back to North Carolina in January. His funeral was originally planned for January 25, but was delayed by severe weather. It was postponed to February 12 and then to February 19 by another snow storm. Wilson was finally buried in the Old Town Cemetery on February 26, 1848. The *Raleigh Standard* of February 28, 1848 recalled:

> The remains of our late Col. Wilson were deposited in the courthouse for three weeks before he was buried. The Saturday before last was the day appointed for the burial, but there was a large snow so it was postponed. . . . I have never seen so long a procession in all my life. They had Frank Johnston's band here to play.

The *Tarborough Press* reported that the crowd numbered between three and four thousand, including people from several surrounding counties. The procession went from the Grove, down Main Street, to the old church. The Reverends J.F. Speight and T.R. Owen delivered the eulogies. Wilson was then laid to rest with Masonic and military honors.

To honor its native son, in 1850 Edgecombe County erected a monument to Wilson on the corner of the Courthouse Square. Tarboro citizens changed the name of St. Joshua Street to Wilson Street. In 1855, the North Carolina Legislature created Wilson County from parts of Edgecombe, Nash, Johnston, and Wayne Counties. Wilson's body was moved to his family cemetery outside of town sometime later. In 1904, the monument at the courthouse had to be relocated, and Wilson was again reburied on the town common with the monument placed over his grave.

TRANSPORTATION

Residents of Edgecombe County had four basic means of transportation in the first half of the nineteenth century: horseback, stagecoach, boat, and railroad. Early settlers used small boats to travel up river from the coast, or migrated south from Virginia using horses and wagons over rough roadways.

By the 1830s, several stage lines were running through Tarboro on a regular basis. Stages operated from Enfield to Tarboro, Rocky Mount to Tarboro, and New Bern to Tarboro, carrying passengers and mail. The Enfield route continued north through Halifax to Petersburg. The Rocky Mount route intersected with routes to Norfolk and Fayetteville, then continued on to Raleigh. In the 1850s, the roads to Rocky Mount and Williamston were made into plank roads. Eventually plank roads or improved roads went to Jamesville, Enfield, Wilson, and Wilmington.

Flat bottom boats were used to transport crops down river and bring some supplies up river from Washington. During the American Revolution, Robert Bignall sent tobacco, naval stores, and other supplies to the Continental Army. The first steamboat to arrive in Tarboro was the *E.D. McNair* in May 1836. Captain Chamberlain brought from Washington the 85-foot steamer with its 20-horsepower engine. Local people boarded the steamer and traveled to Sparta and back. The *McNair* continued to transport goods up and down the river until 1839. In 1847, the *Wayne* began a regular route back and forth along the river. This

A cargo boat sends goods down the Tar River under the old bridge that connected Tarboro and Princeville. This bridge was replaced in 1934. (Courtesy of Edgecombe County Memorial Library.)

steamer was destroyed by fire on the Neuse River near New Bern in 1848. The *Oregon* began travelling the Tar River in 1848, as did the *Governor Graham*. The latter was the largest ship thus far, over 125 feet long and 37 feet wide with two 30-horsepower engines. When the *Wayne* went down in 1848, the *Graham* was sent to the Neuse River.

The *Amidas* first appeared in Tarboro in September 1849. She encountered obstructions in the river just north of Greenville and was damaged. The boat was repaired and appeared in Tarboro in November 1849, towing four flat boats packed with supplies. The *Amidas* was also involved in an incident on the Tar River near the Sparta bridge in 1854. The steamer damaged the bridge and the community wanted to stop the *Amidas* from operating on the river. Another steamer operating on the Tar in the 1850s was the *Governor Morehead*. Steamers continued to transport goods along the Tar River until the Civil War. Once the war was over, steamboat travel continued with paddle wheelers that remained in use well into the early twentieth century.

The Wilmington to Weldon Railroad was completed in 1840. The rails were connected near Rocky Mount and a depot was built there. Another depot was further south at Toisnot, which later became Wilson. A spur line connected Rocky Mount to Tarboro in 1860. By the beginning of the next century, rail transportation replaced much of the river business.

Mr. Henry Britt waits at the Tarboro depot with his crate of pure-bred Rhode Island Reds to transport to a buyer in South America. (Courtesy of Blount-Bridgers House Archives.)

This cotton press—now located on the western edge of the Tarboro town common—was probably built in the 1840s and stood on the Norfleet farm, about 2 miles west of Tarboro. At the peak of cotton production in the 1850s, there were probably a dozen or more such presses in the county. This is the last surviving one in North Carolina.

THE 1850S

The 1850s were very prosperous years for Edgecombe County. Cotton production tripled, new homes and churches were constructed, and the river ports of Sparta and Tarboro were increasing their trade of exported goods—especially naval stores. The number of public schools and the enrollment in all schools increased as education became more important. Industries became more numerous, but agriculture was still the most significant economic endeavor.

The county had seven recognized post offices in 1851: Tarboro with postmaster Samuel Moore, Sparta with postmaster John Hughes, Battleboro with postmaster J.W. Ricks, Rocky Mount with postmaster Malachi Weston, Joyner's Depot with postmaster W.G. Sharp, Wilson with postmaster E.G. Clark, and Stantonsburg with postmaster J.H. Adams. When Wilson County was formed in 1855, these last two post offices became part of that county.

The 1850 federal census for Edgecombe County included six schedules: population, slave, mortality, agriculture, industry, and social statistics. The total population was 17,174, including just over 9,000 slaves owned by 775 slave owners and over 270 free blacks. Typical of the state average, less than 10 percent

The Primitive Baptist congregation established their church in 1819. In the 1850s, they built this structure, which is still used today. Primitive Baptist is the oldest continuous congregation in Tarboro.

of the county's white population owned slaves, and most slave owners averaged five or fewer slaves. The population increased by over 1,500 since the 1840 census. The social statistics indicated that there was no public library in the county. The only newspaper was *The Tarboro Press*, with a circulation of 250. There were 43 public schools—each with its own teacher, each averaging 30 students—funded by a pupil fund, the local school tax. There were four private academies with a total of six teachers, each averaging 40 students who paid tuition.

There were 19 churches in the county: ten Reformed Baptist churches, one Missionary Baptist, four Methodist churches, three Free Baptist churches, and one Episcopal church. The various buildings accommodated 200 to 400 members. Several of these churches expanded during this decade and constructed new and larger buildings. The Primitive Baptist Church built a new structure on the corner of St. James Street and Albemarle Avenue in 1855. St. James Methodist in Tarboro completed a new building in 1856 on the corner of St. James and St. Andrew Streets. Calvary Episcopal Church began a new building in 1858, but the construction was delayed because of the Civil War.

The cemetery around Calvary Church was referred to as "our village 'Garden Tomb' " in a March 27, 1852 article in the newly-named *Tarboro Southerner*. The rector of the parish, Dr. Joseph Blount Cheshire, was an amateur botanist who cultivated many varieties of plants not native to the area. The result was an unusual and inviting arboretum atmosphere. The article continued:

In our beauteous little Church-yard, many useful lessons are taught. The numerous marble mementos with their speaking devices which dot its surface, entreat for the sake of their own truthfulness, purity of life. Consecrated, like the stone erected by Jacobs, they should mark only the spots whence ascended the angels to their home. The bright, beautiful plots of evergreens and flowers—the manifestations of the rarified, spiritual taste of our parson—speak, as himself, to the noblest, purest impulses of our nature.

The eighteen industries in the county included eight turpentine distilleries that produced turpentine and naval stores. Other businesses included a furniture factory, two timber mills, and several grist mills. The largest employer was Battle Cotton Mills, which employed 70, including 50 women. There were almost 900 names listed on the agriculture schedule amongst the county's 540 farms. The average monthly wage of a farm hand was $6.50 with board; day laborers could earn 50¢ a day without board. Female domestics earned 50¢ a week with board. Carpenters could earn over a $1.25 a day.

The construction of homes north of town provided a need for carpenters and brick masons. Louis Wilson broke up the original Blount property and sold off sections west of Main Street as early as the 1830s. The lots went from St. George

*The 1850 and 1860 census industrial schedules listed over a dozen turpentine distilleries in Edgecombe County. The abundance of pine trees made the process of making turpentine very profitable. (*Frank Leslie's Illustrated Newspaper, *September 19, 1866.)*

Street (now Main Street) west to either Hendricks Creek or Creek Street (now Albemarle Avenue). The first few lots were acquired by the Pender family. Solomon Pender completed his home in the 1830s. A son, J.J.B. Pender, built his house in the 1840s and sold it to J.J. Porter in 1854. In the 1840s, Henry Hyman purchased one of the large lots and built Magnolia Hall in the Greek Revival style. In the 1850s, Lyman Dunne and Robert Norfleet both purchased lots on the west side of Main Street and constructed their villas. The Norfleet home included some painted ceilings by Bavarian fresco painter Edward Zoeller. Perhaps the most noticed home in the Tarboro vicinity was the Barracks, built between 1858 and 1860 by William Smith Battle. Designed by architect William Percival, the Barracks was considered by many to be the finest home in town.

An article in the May 24, 1851 edition of the *Tarboro Press* described numerous changes in Tarboro:

> In the town, Mr. Nathan Mathewson has erected a beautiful and elegant building in the cottage style, opposite the Bank—William F. Dancy, Esq., is erecting a spacious building opposite Cotton's Store—and Mr. James S. Pender is enlarging and improving the Hotel, and purposes making it one of the most splendid and convenient public houses in the State.
>
> In the vicinity of town, The Grove, late the property of Col. Wilson, has Passed into the hands of John L. Bridgers, Esq., and Mr. Solomon Pender. Mr. Bridgers has much improved The Grove buildings, and has

Robert Norfleet, a successful merchant in Tarboro, built this suburban villa in 1858 between the Pender and Philips properties. An article in the September 11, 1858 Tarboro Southerner *described the home as a "large one story dwelling, raised some 7 or 8 feet from the ground with 70 feet front, and when completed, it will be one of the finest and best arranged private residences in the state."*

John H. Vines and his wife Prudence Ruffin built this house in the mid-1850s in southern Edgecombe County. Known today as Vinedale, this home passed down through the family for over 100 years. The farm still has several of its original dependencies. It is now the home of Norris Tolson, a former state representative and secretary of transportation in North Carolina.

disposed of part of his land to his brother, Robert R. Bridgers, Esq., who proports improving his part also.

Col. H.T. Clark has purchased that part of the Hunter tract of land on the north side of the road leading by Mr. Shirley's and is busily engaged in collection materials for the erection of buildings on it.

Numerous fine homes appeared throughout the county in the 1850s. Vinedale, near Pinetops, was completed by the Vines family. The Eagles built a fine home in Crisp also south of Tarboro. John and Elizabeth Speight built the Cedars near Speight's Chapel. Dr. James J. Phillips expanded his home, Mount Moriah, in the northern part of the county near Battleboro. Family history indicates that much of the work on the home (featuring beautiful marble mantels) was done by a skilled slave carpenter named Turner Horne. North of Tarboro, Dr. Powell built Coolmore, which is still recognized as one of the finest Italianate villas in the state.

Edgecombe County had a Medical Society in the 1850s with 11 area doctors as members. The Agricultural Society—originally established in the early 1800s—was revived and had 40 members in 1850. The Sons of Temperance No. 202 had 70 active members. Another chapter, No. 77, was in the Temperance Hall area. Other organizations included the International Order of the Odd

Mount Moriah, built in the late 1820s, was the home of Dr. James J. Philips. The house was remodeled in the 1850s with the interior featuring marble mantels and extensive carved woodwork. (Courtesy of North Carolina Office of Archives and History.)

Fellows and four Masonic lodges with a total membership of 176. One of the lodges was located at Mount Moriah, the home of Dr. James J. Philips. The lodge was created by the North Carolina Assembly in 1827 as Mount Moriah Lodge #93. Later, the Masonic building was used as school for the Philips's children and their neighbors.

Tarboro continued to grow throughout the 1850s. An article in the May 23, 1857 Tarboro paper described changes in the town and the nearby countryside:

> Commencing at the upper end of Main street, Mr. H. Blair Bryan's beautiful new building has been purchased for $8,500 and is now occupied by Dr. F.M. Garrett—and Mr. Bryan has purchased for $17,000 and removed to the fertile farm of Mr. Joshua L. Lawrence, containing about 1,000 acres.
>
> Next to Dr. Garrett's is the residence of Mr. J.J.B. Pender, which has been enlarged and improved. Opposite to this is the residence of Mr. R.H. Pender from which the storehouse was been removed and considerable additions and amendments made to the residence. Next to this is the spacious mansion of Dr. J. Lawrence.
>
> Mrs. Nancy Hunter has purchased for $2,700 and occupies part of the block formerly owned by Mr. James Weddell, and has been erected upon

it a neat millinery store, opposite Mrs. Gregory's Hotel—on the other part, Messrs. Weddell and Hart have erected a neat commodious new Storehouse, and part of the lot next to it has been purchased by Mr. Robert Norfleet from Mr. W.H. Powell for $1,750 now occupied by Dr. Garrett's office and Mr. Sizner's Sadlery and harness store.

Below the Court House, the old Brick Store is occupied by Messrs. R.T. Hoskins and Bowditch, merchants, and Mrs. Martha E. Bond, milliner and dressmaker. Next to this building is Mr. Colin Macnair's new store occupied in a clothing house by Messers. A. Feldenheimer and Co. Then comes Mr. F.L. Bond's Furniture Wareroom, which has also been improved and extended.

Proceeding down the street where "Howard's square front" formerly stood, now we behold the new jewelry store of Mr. T.M. Cook, erected by Capt. W.S. Duggan—the second floor occupied by Mr. R.H. Rowe, as Billiard Saloon, and fitted it up in a commodious and elegant style.

Next to this, Messrs. Parker and Lane occupy the building recently erected by Mr. J.S. Pender, which they occupy as a grocery. Dr. Lawrence's office comes next—then the neat little building occupied by Mrs. Julia Bell as millinery and mantumaking establishment; and Mr. David Neal has purchased the corner building from Mr. J.J.B. Pender and occupies it as a boarding house.

Below Messrs. Matthewson and Pippen's storehouse Mr. T.M. Cook occupies the beautiful little building recently erected by J.H. Allen, which he purchased for $1,350—and on the corner next to the Bridge, Capt. Wiley Walston has erected a commodious and beautiful residence.

On Mill Creek street, Messrs. O'berry have in successful operation a steam saw and grist mill, which is a great convenience to the citizens, as well.

As to the surrounding country, and Mr. Green O'berry is now building a new residence near the mill.

The new Primitive Baptist church is also located on this street near the residence of Mr. C.E. Neal, who occupies the two lots formerly owned by Dr. Hall, dec'd. and Mr. John O. Moore has erected a dwelling nearly opposite the Baptist church.

On St. Andrew's street, east of the Court House, the new and spacious Methodist church is erected on the lot next to the residence of Mr. R.H. Austin—and below Mr. Austin's Mr. G.B. Lipscombe has erected two neat and commodious family residences. These, with the splendid residences of Mrs. C. Dancy, W.F. Dancy, Esq., Mr. N. Mathewson, Mr. J.H. Bowditch, and Mrs. C. Williams, render this quite an attractive street.

Several other improvements have taken place in our vicinity, among them Mrs. Foxhall and Mr. Baker Staton's residences merit particular notice. In every direction throughout our county, rapid improvements in agriculture, and in building of elegant and substantial structures are manifesting themselves.

In addition to the progress in business and buildings, there were also political changes in the county. The Compromise of 1850 did not receive popular support in Edgecombe County. With the November 22, 1851 issue of the local paper, publisher George Howard Jr. announced a name change to better reflect the political principles of the county:

> To the People of Edgecombe
>> The "Tarboro Press" will be discontinued at the close of this year.
>> By the above article it will be seen that with the present year terminates the career of the "Press." With the next, the subscriber hopes to begin the *Southerner* in an enlarged and improved form, advocating the same principles and issued on the same terms.
>> We selected the name of "*Southerner*" with no design of appearing sectional, at least, we use it not as contradistinguished from American or Union; for we honestly believe that the day in which our present plan of Government or Union is abandoned, the American people retrograde in liberty and glory at least half a century.
>> The cause of discontent is entirely under the regulation of the North, if they rest contented now, the Union is perpetual; but should they choose to give it another impetus, let them answer for its terrible effects.

Agriculture remained the economic source for the county. The Agricultural Society from the early part of the century was revived. Crops included cotton, corn, and wheat. A new type of tobacco was being planted in limited quantities near Conetoe. Of the 840 farms in Edgecombe County in 1850, 62 were over 1.000 acres in size and a third of those were over 2,000 acres. Twelve of the largest plantations ranged between 2,500 and 6,000 acres. The land owners of the larger plantations each owned from 35 to more than 200 slaves.

Cotton was the dominant crop in Edgecombe County. Although the 1850 census indicated that the cotton crop of 1849 was down 20 percent from the usual average of 5,000 bales, that soon changed as more cotton was planted and new methods increased yield. Much of the cotton used in the Battle mill was locally grown. In 1840, Edgecombe ranked fifth in North Carolina—after Anson, Northampton, Columbus, and Halifax Counties—producing over 2 million pounds of cotton per year. According to a report in the June 18, 1851 paper, the county "produced 1,528 bales weighing 400 pounds each" in 1840. By 1849, production had increased to 3,300 bales. The next year, the cotton crop exceeded 5,000 bales.

There were several cotton presses on large farms throughout the county. After seeds were removed in the cotton gins, the presses formed the cotton into bales. One press survives on the town common, moved there from the Norfleet farm.

By the Civil War, Edgecombe County was producing more cotton than any other county in the state, averaging over 7 million pounds per year.

Cotton was not just a profitable crop. Picking cotton became a contest among some slaves and slave owners. Various issues of the *Tarboro Southerner* in the 1850s (including October 11, 1851) reported on the outcome of such competitions.

> *Mr. Howard*: I send you for publication the quantity of seed cotton picked on Mr. Richard Hine's plantation in this county, yesterday, the 7th inst by six hands.—they commenced picking at light in the morning and continued until dusk, just time to see to weigh without a light. Sacks were used by all the hands except the two first named, who from three o'clock in the evening until night two small boys to move their baskets.—previous to that time they used sacks. The whole of the cotton was weighed by me, and the result is as follows:
>
> Herbert, 627 lbs. / Isaac, 598 / Nicey, 475 14 years old / Mima, 421 / Little Jim, 430 / Fanny, 410.
>
> Making in all 2961 lbs and averaging 493 1/2 lbs. to each hand.
>
> Jesse H. Powell.
>
> Oct. the 8th, 1851.

Similar reports came from various county plantations each fall. In a competition between the slaves of Baker Staton of Cotton Valley and J.S. Dancy

In the 1920s, Edgecombe County had over 70 schools, including this one, Chinquapin, located in the southeast section. Education may have been important, but cotton fields reflect the dominance of agriculture in the region. (Courtesy of North Carolina Office of Archives and History.)

of Panola, all picked over 400 pounds. Another competition on the farm of J.L. Horn at Town Creek involved slaves from John Mercer's and Robert Bridgers's plantations, who averaged 485 pounds each. This was followed by a report from Elijah Nevill on Old Tar River of an average 536 pounds. The earlier records all fell in September 1858, when an "extraordinary Cotton Picking" was held at R.R. Bridgers's Strabane plantation. The October 9, 1858 the *Tarboro Southerner* reported:

> Thirty-two "hands" picked sixteen thousand and ninety-six pounds being an average of 503 lbs.—the highest, a man named Herbert, picked one thousand and sixty seven pounds—the four highest averaged seven hundred and seventy nine and one–fourth pounds, the fourteen highest averaged six hundred and nine and one half pounds. . . . During the afternoon Herbert picked seventy-seven pounds in fifty-five minutes.

The winters of 1856 and 1857 had especially active weather. The January 19, 1856 newspaper reported:

> On Saturday last we had another fall of snow to the depth of three or four inches. The former snow had not disappeared, and as the weather continues cold, a fine opportunity is afforded our citizens for enjoying the delightful amusements of slipping and sliding, sleighing, skating, and snow balling.

The following week another snow was recorded, "being the third within the past three weeks." It snowed again in February, and March saw two more snowfalls. The second, reported on March 29, 1856, was "several snow storms, with awful claps of thunder, some rain winding up with ice of quarter of an inch thick next morning." The final snow of 1856 came over two days in April with "several light falls which melted nearly as fast as it fell but the ground froze and ice half an inch thick did much damage to gardens.

The next winter was not much better. The January 24, 1857 paper reported more snow and cold weather:

> On Sunday last, we had a severe snowstorm, the snow falling to the depth of some ten or twelve inches. The weather continuing extremely cold, our youthful population had a fine opportunity of enjoying the northern sports of sleigh riding, snow balling, &c. On Tuesday, the thermometer stood at 2 degrees above zero, the coldest weather known in these parts. Tar river frozen over, navigation suspended. On Wednesday night another fall of snow, two or three inches deep, the weather yet extremely cold. On Thursday, the thermometer 5 degrees below zero. Whew!

3. War and Recovery
1860–1880

The 20 years between 1860 to 1880 brought tremendous change in Edgecombe County: many died in the war that tore the country apart; those with property lost it, and those without freedom received it. The economics, politics, and educational opportunities all shifted. The planter class lost the most in terms of lifestyle, while the slaves gained the most. Slaves outnumbered whites by almost two to one (6,789 whites, 389 free blacks, 10,108 slaves), so their freedom and enfranchisement caused a major power shift. The smaller farms contributed most of the soldiers who filled over six companies; more than 1,400 men and boys from Edgecombe County served in the Confederate Army.

The county had grown in the 1850s, but with no significant differences from the 1850 census. The overall population of 17,376 changed very little, and its increase was in the slave and free black populations. The number of churches decreased to 15, but the Baptists were still the dominant sect, followed by Methodists and Episcopalians. There was a decrease in public schools from 43 to 34, and an increase in private schools from 4 to 13. One major change was in libraries. In the previous census, there were no known libraries in the county. By 1860, there were six private libraries—including three law collections and one medical library—with over 1,000 volumes. There was also a change in public awareness. A second paper, *The Tarboro Mercury*, competed with the *Tarboro Southerner*. Its weekly circulation climbed to almost 1,800, compared to the more established paper's 300.

The biggest change over the previous decade was in transportation and industry. Ten years earlier, the 18 businesses relied on river transportation or stagecoaches. That changed when a spur line of the Wilmington & Weldon Railroad from Rocky Mount to Tarboro opened in the summer of 1860. The number and types of businesses also changed. There were over three dozen businesses: many were saw mills, but none were turpentine distilleries. There were also more wheel wrights and blacksmiths. New industry included three brickyards, one gunsmith, and one photographer. To reflect the need for skilled workers, wages had doubled to $12 per month for a farm hand and $1 per week for a domestic worker. The building spurt of the late 1850s, however, was halted by the war as many men went off to fight.

In late 1860, North Carolinians were divided regarding the outcome of the presidential election and the secession of South Carolina. Democrat John C. Breckinridge received 1,217 votes in Edgecombe County. Abraham Lincoln was not even on the ballot in North Carolina. The state legislature voted on a convention bill in January 1861 to consider secession. John Bridgers of Edgecombe County led the radicals who supported secession, but at the February convention, the conservatives won and North Carolina voted to stay in the Union. Regardless, the desire of Edgecombe was made clear: over 1,500 of 1,600 voters wanted to leave the Union and join the Confederacy. In early February, North Carolina sent three delegates to meet with the new Confederate government that had formed in Alabama. Former governor David L. Swain, Matt

John Luther Bridgers, lawyer and businessman, was captain of the Edgecombe Guards and led that company in the battle of Big Bethel, Virginia in June 1861. Bridgers was also commandant at Fort Macon. He lived in the Grove until 1881. (Courtesy of Blount-Bridgers House Archives.)

Ransom of Warren County, and John L. Bridgers of Edgecombe were sent to observe the meeting, but could not participate nor vote.

In the next two months, as tensions mounted throughout the nation, Edgecombe residents met with other Southern rights supporters in Wilson and in Goldsboro. In early April, they held their own meeting in Tarboro. The wealthy plantation owners constituted less than 10 percent of the farmers, yet owned over 60 percent of the slaves. They opposed Lincoln and abolition and were prepared to go war. Smaller farmers and many non-slave owners also were convinced that joining the Confederacy was the practical thing to do.

Two events on April 14, 1861 impacted Edgecombe County and local families. First, Fort Sumter was surrendered to the Confederates in Charleston, South Carolina. The country was at war, but North Carolina remained in the Union. Second, Fort Macon on the North Carolina coast was captured by members of the Beaufort Guards. Captain Josiah Pender, a native of Edgecombe County, led a small group across the sound from Beaufort to Fort Macon. They captured the federal garrison without a single shot: the lone guard surrendered without a fight. Pender's capture of the fort was the first military action in the state, even though North Carolina was still a part of the Union.

After the fall of Fort Sumter, President Lincoln sent a request to North Carolina Governor John Ellis, asking for troops to help put down the rebellion. For the next hundred years, many school children were taught the governor's reply, "you will get no troops from North Carolina." The request and reply instead inspired thousands of North Carolinians to volunteer for the Confederate forces, and Edgecombe County was no exception. On May 21, 1861, North Carolina officially left the Union and joined the Confederacy. Several companies of its men were already drilling, in preparation for war and protection of the home front.

Governor Ellis, though suffering from poor health, began plans to protect the state. Because North Carolina was the last state to join the Confederacy, it had little recognition in the early Confederate government. Ellis was concerned with protecting the residents of his state and defending its land, especially along the coast, from the Union Navy that had been blockading since mid-April. Ellis also appointed Dr. Charles Johnson as surgeon general of North Carolina. Dr. Johnson quickly set up a hospital on the state fair grounds in Raleigh and created a system of wayside hospitals throughout the state to take care of the anticipated sick and wounded soldiers. The wayside hospitals were set up in towns with rail lines, so troops could be transported to their facilities.

Two of the wayside hospitals were set up in Tarboro and Wilson. Tarboro was probably selected over Rocky Mount because it was much larger in population, it had sites that could serve as hospitals, and its spur line was the eastern most point of the railway. The specific site chosen was the Tarboro Academy located on Hendricks Creek on the western edge of town. As the war progressed, the Female Academy on the eastern end of the common was also turned into a hospital. Although there are no complete existing records of the schools or the hospitals, presumably the schools closed for the duration of the war.

Made in Edenton around 1800 by cabinetmaker William Manning, this handsome desk belonged to Henry Toole Clark, a resident of Tarboro and governor of North Carolina during the Civil War.

GOVERNOR HENRY TOOLE CLARK

In the summer of 1861, Governor John Ellis died. At the time, North Carolina did not have a lieutenant governor. The next in line to fill the governor's seat was the speaker of the state senate, Henry Toole Clark of Tarboro. Clark was the son of James West Clark who had served in the Jackson administration. His ancestors were some of the earliest settlers in the county, and he lived most of his life in Tarboro in a house still standing on St. Patrick Street. Clark attended Louisburg Academy before graduating from the University of North Carolina at age 18. Afterwards, he practiced law and managed the family plantation. In 1850, he married a widowed cousin, Mary Weeks Hargrave. Clark was elected to his first seat in the state government that same year and served in the state legislature for the next decade.

As governor, Clark continued with Ellis's plans to protect his state. He prepared for war by raising troops and regulating their necessary supplies and equipment. He requested that the Confederacy allow some North Carolina troops to remain in the state to protect its coast from a possible invasion. That request was denied

and most North Carolina troops—including many from Edgecombe—were sent
to the Army of Northern Virginia. Governor Clark's fears were realized as the
North Carolina coast fell into Union hands. After a short term of just over a year,
Clark refused to run in the 1862 election. A new governor, Zebulon Vance, led the
state for the remainder of the war.

Henry Clark retired to Hilma, his plantation just west of Tarboro. During the
war, he met with Governor Vance in Tarboro and also defended the town from a
Union raid in July 1863. After the war, he served one term in the state senate. He
spent his last years researching and writing North Carolina history and genealogy.
He died exactly nine years after President Lincoln's assassination, on April 15,
1874, and was buried in Calvary Churchyard.

Edgecombe Troops

When North Carolina seceded, thousands of men across the state volunteered to
serve in either the home guard or the Confederate Army. During the four years of
war, Edgecombe county provided 1,400 soldiers—most were volunteers, but a
few were conscripted when the war lasted longer than expected. The Edgecombe
Guards became Company A of the 1st North Carolina Infantry Regiment; the
Edgecombe Rifles became Company G of the 13th N.C. Regiment; the
Confederate Guards became Company I of the 15th N.C. Regiment; the Rocky
Mount Light Infantry became Company K of the 15th N.C. Regiment; the
Edgecombe Rebels became Company I of the 17th N.C. Regiment; the Spartan
Band became Company F of the 30th N.C. Regiment; Clark's Guards became
Company B of the 33rd N.C. Regiment; Captain Lloyd's Light Artillery became
Company G of the 40th N.C. Regiment; and Captain Vine's company became
Company E of the 43rd N.C. Regiment.

Edgecombe soldiers also made up part of several other North Carolina
regiments, but not in large enough numbers to provide an entire company of 100
or more men. Some served in the 8th, 44th, and 75th N.C. Regiments; others
joined companies from neighboring counties, including several units from
Halifax, Nash, and Wilson Counties. Edgecombe County soldiers engaged in
most battles in Virginia and several in eastern North Carolina. Two companies are
detailed in books: Craig Chapman's *More Terrible than Victory* recounts the history
of the North Carolina 1st Regiment, including the Edgecombe Guards, and
Michael Taylor's *To Drive the Enemy from Southern Soil* describes the 30th N.C.
Regiment and the Spartan Band.

The Edgecombe Guards—a unit that had been in operation since the 1830s as
a local militia—joined the 1st North Carolina Regiment under the command of
Daniel H. Hill. The unit was assigned to southern Virginia and played a
prominent role in the Battle of Bethel on June 10, 1861. John L. Bridgers served
as captain to the 130 Edgecombe men. Whitmel P. Lloyd, grandson of Mary Lloyd
Gregory, was first lieutenant and later replaced Bridgers as captain. William
Gaston Lewis of Rocky Mount was second lieutenant and became major general

by the end of the war. Non-commissioned officers included Thigpen, Staton, Palamountain, Cotton, and Cobb. One volunteer Henry Wyatt, age 19, was an apprenticed carpenter who worked at the Bond cabinet factory.

At the Battle of Bethel, the North Carolina regiment was outnumbered four to one by Union forces under command of Benjamin Butler. Volunteers were called to take a house occupied by snipers. Wyatt led the charge towards the house, only to be shot in the head—the first North Carolinian to die in battle. The Union suffered 18 losses and over 50 wounded. The Confederates lost Wyatt along with nine wounded. After the battle, Wyatt's remains were taken to his mother's family in Richmond, and he was interred in the Hollywood Cemetery there. The 1st North Carolina was renamed the Bethel Regiment in honor of this skirmish.

Because many of the volunteers had only signed up for six months, the regiment was reorganized in late November 1861. In the spring of 1862, the men were reassigned to McLaw's Division in the Army of Northern Virginia. They participated in most battles in eastern Virginia, including Seven Pines, Seven Days, Sharpsburg, Fredericksburg, Chancellorsville, Gettysburg, the Wilderness, Spotsylvania, North Anna, Cold Harbor, and the Petersburg siege, which ended with the surrender at Appomattox.

West Point graduate William Dorsey Pender was the first commander of the 13th North Carolina. He was born in 1834, in what is now Wilson County, the son of James Pender. One of nine children, William was the only son not to

This statue of Henry Lawson Wyatt on the capital grounds in Raleigh recognizes him as the first North Carolina soldier to die in the Civil War. A volunteer in the Edgecombe Guards, which became Company B of the First North Carolina Regiment, he was killed on June 10, 1861 in the battle of Big Bethel, Virginia.

In the early twentieth century, local citizens were active in several organizations to remember past residents and ancestors who were in the American Revolution or the Civil War. This fountain was installed on the town common in 1904 to commemorate Henry Wyatt, the first Confederate soldier to die in combat in the Civil War.

become a farmer (like his father) or a merchant (like his brothers). He graduated from West Point in 1854 and served in the U.S. Army until the war, whereupon he resigned his commission and joined the Confederate Army. Just before the war, Pender married Mary "Fanny" Shepherd, the sister of one of his West Point classmates. When the war began, William and Fanny had one son and were expecting a second. Pender's love for his wife has been preserved in a series of letters to her, which were published almost 100 years after his death.

The Bethel Regiment was part of Colston's Brigade, Longstreet's Division, and saw action at the battle of Seven Pines. The regiment was then transferred to Garland's Brigade in D.H. Hill's Division and fought in the Seven Days campaign and Sharpsburg. In October, the regiment was transferred to Pender's Brigade in A.P. Hill's Division. It was fighting at Fredericksburg in December 1862 when Pender was wounded. The report of the 13th N.C. says:

> Just then Gen. Pender came riding down his line among the hail of shot
> and shells, his left-hand hanging down and blood streaming down his
> fingers. A ball had gone through the arm between the bones. Col. Scales
> bounded up out of the snow and said "General, I see you are wounded."

> He said "Oh, that is a trifle. No bone broken. I want you to send at least two companies down the railroad and drive those scoundrels out."

Pender's wound at Fredericksburg was not serious, but he was wounded again in May 1863 at Chancellorsville. With the death of Stonewall Jackson, Pender was promoted to division commander, but only held that position for a couple of months. After the success over the Union Army at Chancellorsville, Lee decided to move the army north on the offensive. The next major encounter was at the Pennsylvania town of Gettysburg.

William Gaston Lewis, who had been the second lieutenant at Bethel, was a major by Gettysburg. The son of Catherine Battle and Dr. John Lewis, he was named after North Carolina Supreme Court Justice William Gaston. Lewis graduated from the University of North Carolina and worked as a school teacher and an engineer for the railroad prior to the war. Later in a letter in the Southern History Collection at the University of North Carolina, dated 1893, Lewis described to D. Gilliam a meeting with Pender:

> I called on him at his headquarters and though I was much inferior in rank, he then being Brig. Gen. He received me most cordially and courteously, and I had a very pleasant visit, and one of profit to me, as I saw plainly in his camps the results of true military discipline and careful attention from Headquarters. His camp was a model of cleanliness, regularity and good order.

According to Lewis, he, Pender, and Major Joseph Englehard:

> were having a pleasant conversation when all of a sudden the enemy opened fire with 350 pieces of artillery . . . directly on our line on Seminary Ridge. The air was full of exploding shells and shell and solid shot were knocking the granite boulders into small rocks and scattering them over us. Pender received a wound in the thigh.

General William Dorsey Pender was removed from the field and transported to a field hospital. After several days, his left leg was amputated. A telegram was sent to his family in Tarboro and Pender's brother David visited him in the hospital at Staunton, Virginia. Shortly after his brother arrived, and two weeks after being wounded, Pender died of gangrene on July 18, 1863. David escorted his brother's remains to Tarboro and interred them in Calvary Churchyard. A marker was not put on his gravesite for many years, but today it is surrounded by cannonballs and inscribed: "Patriot by nature, soldier by training, Christian by faith." Pender's wife Fanny delivered their third son in September. His former regiment, the 13th, was transferred for the last time to Scales' Brigade in May 1863. They saw action at Gettysburg, the Wilderness, Spotsylvania, and the Petersburg siege, before surrendering at Appomattox.

The 15th N.C. Regiment served in both North Carolina and in the Army of Northern Virginia as part of Ransom's Division. These units fought at Seven Days, Harpers Ferry, Sharpsburg, Fredericksburg, Cold Harbor, Hatcher's Run, and Petersburg, among others, before surrendering at Appomattox. The 17th N.C. spent most of the war protecting North Carolina. It was assigned to Martin's Brigade in the Department of North Carolina and later to Hoke's Division. It served at first Plymouth in December 1862 and at Williamston and Tarboro in 1863. In the summer of 1864, it was assigned to the Army of Northern Virginia and fought at Bermuda Hundred and Cold Harbor. It was then reassigned to North Carolina to the Cape Fear District and fought at Fort Fisher, Wise Forks, and Bentonville. The last assignment was with the Army of Tennessee, which surrendered at Bennett Place in Durham.

The commander of the 30th North Carolina was Colonel Francis Marion Parker. He led the regiment until he was wounded at Spotsylvannia in May 1864. Parker was the son of Tarboro merchant and bank president Theophilus Parker and his wife Mary Irwin Toole. Frank Parker, as he was locally known, grew up in the family home on Church Street. His first cousin was Henry Toole Clark, governor during the war. Parker's sister married Joseph Cheshire, rector of

David Pender, brother of General William Dorsey Pender, built this Greek Revival home on Main Street just north of the town common in the early 1860s. The porch features elaborate Italianate-style columns. David traveled to Staunton, Virginia to be with his brother Dorsey, who had been wounded at Gettysburg.

Six Edgecombe county veterans attended the 50th anniversary reunion at Gettysburg in 1913. The men are John Whitaker Cotten, who served in Company A of the 40th N.C. Regiment; W.T. Gorham, who served in the 17th N.C.; E.I. Felton of Company F of the 4th N.C.; A.J. David of Company I of the 75th N.C.; Redding Reasons of Company I of the 75th N.C.; and J.B. Vick of Company I of the 75th N.C.

Calvary Church. In 1849, Parker inherited his father's large farm, which included over 900 acres and about 25 slaves. Two years later, Parker married Sarah "Sally" Tart Philips, the daughter of Dr. J.J. Philips of northern Edgecombe County. The Parkers soon moved across Fishing Creek to a new plantation near Enfield. Before the war began, Parker became the second lieutenant of the Enfield Blues, which was part of the 1st N.C. This regiment was reorganized and assigned to the 30th North Carolina, of which Parker was elected colonel on October 7, 1861. His brother-in-law Frederick Philips became Parker's adjutant.

Parker received a head wound on September 17, 1862 at Sharpsburg and again in May 1864 near Spotsylvania. This second wound was serious, but it was a third wound—in the abdomen, received on May 19 at Harris Farm—that forced him home and ended his military service. Parker returned home to his family of nine children. The second child, James Philips Parker, attended the U.S. Naval Academy in 1873 and eventually became a commodore in the navy. Parker and his wife, along with both of their families, were buried in Calvary Churchyard.

The 30th N.C. included the Spartan Band, Company F, and received heavy casualties at Gaines Mill in June 1862; Malvern Hill on July 1, 1862; Sharpsburg in September 1862; Chancellorsville on May 3, 1863; Gettysburg in July, 1863; and Kelly's Ford on November 7, 1863. The heaviest casualties were at Spotsylvania: 31 were killed, 54 wounded, and over 80 captured. The Spartan Band had five killed, four mortally wounded, five wounded, and four captured. The regiment surrendered at Appomattox in April 1865.

Clark's Guards, Company B of the 33rd N.C. Regiment, served under Colonel Lawrence O'Brien Branch, who was originally from Enfield. William Gaston Lewis was also assigned to this regiment. In May 1862, the unit tried to defend New Bern against a Union invasion under command of Ambrose Burnside. After losing the coast of North Carolina to the Union forces, the regiments were reassigned and became a part of A.P. Hill's Division in Northern Virginia. Like other Edgecombe companies, Clark's Guards saw action at Seven Days, Second Bull Run, Harpers Ferry, and Sharpsburg—where they lost their commander. Branch was killed at Sharpsburg on September 17, 1862. A Confederate fort being constructed on the Roanoke River was renamed Fort Branch in his memory. The regiment was engaged in every major battle in Virginia from Fredericksburg to the surrender at Appomattox. Company B was one of the dozens of North Carolina units at Gettysburg, and it received heavy casualties. An incomplete casualty list in the July 23, 1863 *Raleigh State Journal* identified over 44 men from Edgecombe County as killed, wounded, or missing; 16 were from Company B of the 33rd.

Company G of the 40th N.C. was commanded by Whitmel P. Lloyd, who had also been part of the Bethel Regiment. Prior to the war, Lloyd married Harriet Howard, the daughter of the publisher of the Tarboro newspaper. After delivering their third child, Harriet died in 1861. Although other companies of the 40th N.C. fought in several North Carolina skirmishes and battles, Company G was assigned to the Artillery Battalion of D.H. Hill's Division and fought in the battle of Sharpsburg on September 17, 1862. Lloyd survived the war and returned home to Tarboro, where he married Laura Frances Pender, a niece of Capt. Josiah Pender.

Company E of the 43rd N.C was the remaining unit of mostly Edgecombe County men. The original commander was Thomas S. Kenan, who was killed at Gettysburg. Command was then given to William Gaston Lewis, originally of the Bethel Regiment. This company was assigned to Daniel's Brigade until his death at Spotsylvania. General Junius Daniel was a native of nearby Halifax. When Daniel was killed in May 1864, command was given to General Bryan Grimes from neighboring Pitt County. Lewis remained with this regiment until he was wounded at Farmville on April 7, 1865. Lewis had a horse shot out from under him, but was saved by a local doctor named Spencer. In his memoirs, Lewis wrote of Spencer,

> My life, whatever it is worth, I owe to him and his care, through kind of Providence that directs the lives of all. It is impossible for me to fully express my thanks to Dr. Spencer. I have named one son for him, whom I sincerely desire shall grow up to be such a man as his namesake. He could not be better.

Lewis returned to Edgecombe County after the war. During a visit home in 1864, he had married Martha "Mittie" Pender, the sister of Whitmel Lloyd's wife, and a cousin of General Dorsey Pender. Lewis returned to his prewar occupation as a civil engineer for the railroad. Between 1866 and 1871, he held various jobs on the North Carolina railroads as engineer and eventually president of the Tarboro to Williamston Railroad. In the 1870s, Lewis lived with his wife and seven children on the corner of Main and Wilson Streets, and operated a hardware store in Tarboro. In 1885, he was appointed state engineer, and moved to Goldsboro, where he died in 1901. His son James Spencer Lewis (named for the doctor who

The North Carolina monument at Gettysburg is dedicated to the thousands of men from the state who fought or died in this battle. Over 1,500 men from Edgecombe County served in the war and many were at Gettysburg.

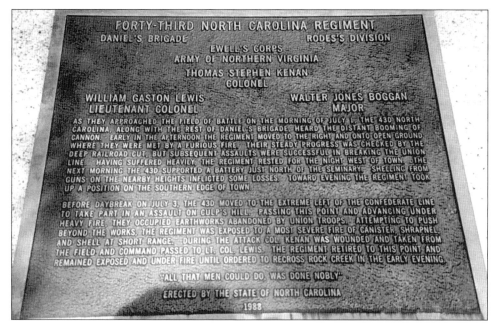

Lieutenant Colonel William Lewis of Edgecombe County, a member of the 43rd North Carolina, took command of that regiment after Colonel Kenan was wounded in battle at Culp's Hill on July 3, 1863. Lewis was later promoted to brigadier general.

saved his father's life) attended the University of North Carolina and served as a sergeant of Company B of the 1st N.C. Volunteers in the Spanish American War.

Dorsey Pender is the most recognized name of local soldiers involved in the war—one of only three county men who became generals, but one of hundreds who died in the war. The other two local generals were the above mentioned William Gaston Lewis and William Ruffin Cox. Cox was from Scotland Neck. He lived and practiced law in Tennessee before the war. In 1856, he returned home and married Penelope Battle. She was the daughter of James Smith Battle, owner of Battle Mills of Rocky Mount. They built a home on their plantation, Penelo, in western Edgecombe County between Tarboro and Rocky Mount. Cox volunteered for service when the war began. He became a major in the 2nd N.C. Regiment and served through the war, being wounded eleven times. He received five wounds at Chancellorsville and recovered at home, thus missing Gettysburg. He returned to duty and after the battle of Spotsylvania, was promoted to brigadier general in charge of the 2nd, 4th, 10th, and 14th N.C. Regiments. He was a brigade commander in Grimes' Division at the end of the war, and it was his brigade that fired the last volley of shots at Appomattox.

After the war, Cox returned to Edgecombe County to raise his family. His first wife Penelope died in 1880. When Cox remarried, he maintained a law office and home in Raleigh. He was president of the Chatham Railroad and became active in state politics. He was a circuit judge from 1876 to 1880. He served in the

William Ruffin Cox, a lawyer from Scotland Neck, built this home in the 1850s for his wife Penelope Battle. The plantation was called Penelo (Courtesy of North Carolina Office of Archives and History.)

United States Senate from 1881 to 1887 and was a strong advocate of civil service reform. He also served as president of the North Carolina State Educational Association and the North Carolina Agricultural Association. Cox died in 1919 at the age of 88—making him one of the longest living Confederate generals—and he was buried in Oakwood Cemetery in Raleigh.

On the base of the North Carolina monument at Appomattox Courthouse in Virginia are engraved these words: "First at Bethel, / Farthest to the front Gettysburg and at Chickamauga, / Last at Appomattox." It is often referred to as the Carolina Boast because North Carolinians were involved in the first battle, gained the most ground during the Pickett-Pettigrew charge at Gettysburg, and fired the final shots before the surrender at Appomattox Courthouse. This could also be the Edgecombe Boast, because soldiers from that County were a part of each of these military distinctions: Bridgers, Lloyd, and Lewis were at Bethel and Wyatt died there; many others from Edgecombe were at Gettysburg and Pender died there; Cox fired the last shots at Appomattox.

WAR IN EDGECOMBE COUNTY

Even though hundreds of local men were far away in Virginia, the war remained close to Edgecombe County. Troops were often moved through the area on the railroad's spur line. William A. Day of Catawba County served in Company I of the 49th North Carolina Regiment. While he saw action at several major battles in Virginia, he also spent part of the war in North Carolina. In 1893, he published his memories of that service:

> On the 11th of August we took the train at Weldon and went to Rocky Mount and from there we marched to Tarboro a distance of eighteen miles and camped in the edge of town. Tarboro is a beautiful town situated on the Tar river and it is the county seat of Edgecombe county, and said to be the wealthiest county in North Carolina. It was in the height of the fruit season and apples, peaches, watermelons, muskmelons and almost everything else in the fruit line were there. The watermelons we had to buy, but the apples and peaches they gave to us. . . . We had a fine time there, nothing to do but walk about the town and bathe in the river. One man in our Regiment concluded he would join the Baptist church and as our chaplain was a Baptist minister, he took him down to the Tar river and baptized him but it didn't do him much good, for in a few days he needed baptizing again. We remained there a week.

Confederate soldiers were not the only ones to visit Tarboro. For a short time, the lens from the Cape Hatteras Lighthouse was hidden in Tarboro to keep it out of Union hands. It was later transported by train to another North Carolina town. However, the Union was able to recover the lens at the end of the war. Twice in less than a year, Union troops advanced towards Edgecombe County, the second time leaving death and destruction. The first raid was in November 1862 and began as a campaign to Tarboro from Plymouth through Williamston and Hamilton and nearby Fort Branch. General John Foster was in command of Union forces, who had set up headquarters in New Bern after the Union victory there in the spring of 1862. Foster was accompanied by 5,000 men who marched from Washington to the west towards Tarboro, where they intended to surprise Confederate forces. They encountered some home guards at Williamston on November 2 and then marched to and destroyed Hamilton, about 20 miles east of Tarboro. Contemporary newspapers and letters reported fires and looting. Leaving Hamilton, Foster's troops marched within 10 miles of Tarboro, but retreated upon hearing of "heavy Confederate troop concentration in the area" (Barrett, p. 138)—apparently train whistles indicating the arrival of troops. Scouts believed that numerous Confederates were being sent to the area to flank Foster's troops, although other sources indicate that the train whistles were actually a bluff. F.L. Bond recorded in his diary that a majority of the regiments—the 17th, 26th, 59th, 44th, 42nd, 56th, and 47th, along with South Carolina regiments—did not appear until November 11. Regardless, Foster retreated to Plymouth, where naval forces returned his troops to New Bern. Bond also recorded that on November 3, "Gov. Vance accompanied by ex-Gov.

Clark, J.L. Bridgers and others crossed the bridge to advise with General Martin as to where this best position would be." (*Tarboro Southerner* Bicentennial ed.)

A second raid was planned for Tarboro in the summer of 1863. "A sizable cavalry force left New Bern and raided Greenville, Tarboro and Rocky Mount" on July 19 under the command of Brigadier General Edward Potter (Barrett, p. 164). After getting drunk in Greenville taverns and burning that bridge over the Tar River, the troops marched to Sparta. They spent part of the night there, then divided forces with one group going to Rocky Mount—where their main objective was to destroy the railroad—and a second group to Tarboro.

Union General Potter arrived in Tarboro around 7 a.m. on July 20 and proceeded to destroy an incomplete ironclad at the docks. Potter reported that "he burned the vessel, along with two steamboats, some railroad equipment, 100 bales of cotton, and a considerable amount of quartermaster goods" (Trotter, p. 204). F.L. Bond made no mention of the ironclad, but did record that Potter's cavalry crossed the bridge and were driven back by Major Kennedy. "They crossed and fired the bridge behind them. The citizens assembled and extinguished the flames. Among them were Philip Garnett, Dr. Joe Baker, Gov. Clark and others." Catherine Devereux Edmondston, mistress of Looking Glass Plantation in neighboring Halifax County, kept a detailed diary of the war years and also mentioned the major:

> Our gratitude is due to Major Kennedy of Griffin's Rangers & to Col. Lamb, 17th NC Troops, who in two separate engagements on different sides of the river repulsed them and hastened their retreat. They were compelled to disgorge a large quantity of their plunder, so severe was the onset made upon them by our troops.

Although no local papers were printed until a month after the raid, a later newspaper reported a witness recalling these details:

> They came by the Wilson Road (St.) and as soon as they crossed the creek they spread out into every street in town. They began to search the houses and when they came to our home my grandmother and I followed them through each room, and I recall that they found the only pistol that I had ever seen to that time. . . . We found out that the officer entered some of the stores and had all the whiskey poured out in the gutters as they feared for the men to drink. They took provisions and such things as they needed, but did no damage to the place. They had burned the commissary and the jail. . . . There came a report that a large force of Confederates were on their way to Tarboro from Plymouth so the Yankees who had arrived before 10 am left before dark. (*Southerner* Bicentennial ed.)

Mrs. Edmondston chronicled the Tarboro raid in her journal for days. Her July 21 entry recorded that:

the enemy have made a sudden advance via Greenville to Tarboro, which they occupy, burning the bridge to prevent Gen. Martin from advancing upon them and cutting off their rear. One column then advanced towards Rocky Mount, which it is rumored they occupy & are tearing up the RR track.

The next day, she recorded, "the enemy have retreated from both Rocky Mount & Tarboro. They burned both factories at the former place destroyed the Telegraph station, the RR bridge, the Depot & some other houses" Not until July 23 did she relate the actual damage in Tarboro:

> The enemy carried off in their late foray into Edgecombe about 500 negroes & a number of horses. They destroyed every vestige of a Gun boat being built at Tarboro, even burning a quantity of timber in the ship yard there. They set the county bridge over the Tar on fire in five places, but our troops were fortunately in time to extinguish it before much damage was done.

James M. Cutchin was born in Edgecombe County in 1841. He enlisted in 1862 in Company I of the 17th North Carolina. He served primarily in North Carolina: at Kinston in 1863, at Plymouth in 1864, and at Bentonville in 1865. Lieutenant Colonel Cutchin was discharged in Greensboro on April 19, 1865 at the end of the war. (Courtesy of North Carolina Office of Archives and History.)

71

Meanwhile, Major Jacobs and six companies of the 3rd New York Cavalry Regiment proceeded to Rocky Mount, where they encountered a train with at least 15 confederate soldiers and supplies, which were destroyed along with:

> the depot, railroad and telegraph offices, country bridge, railroad bridge, cotton mills, [Battle Mills] flour mill, 1000 barrels of flour, hardtack, a machine-shop of munitions, storehouses, [over 30] wagons . . . and over 800 bales of cotton. (Barrett, p. 165–166.)

Fortunately, the 150 mill employees were evacuated before the building was burned. Recorded as the Battle of Daniel's Schoolhouse in Tarboro, several versions of this confrontation exist from Union reports, Confederate regiment histories, and later newspaper reports. Approximately 80 men led by J.B. Edgerton

This grave in Calvary Churchyard marks the resting place of the only naval officer from Edgecombe County to serve in the Confederacy. Ivey Foreman died one day after his 21st birthday in a Richmond Hospital on December 21, 1864.

from Fort Branch attacked Potter's forces from an ambush near Danielhurst—the home of Primitive Baptist Minister John Daniel across the river, south of Tarboro. Accounts vary as to the outcome. The Confederates claim to have mortally wounded two soldiers and captured five prisoners and numerous horses. The Union reported losses of 2 killed, 15 wounded, and 16 prisoners. Later reports described the small skirmish as resulting in six Union soldiers dying. They were brought to town and buried in the Old Town Cemetery until after the war, when their remains were returned to their families.

Although the Union troops set fire to the Tar River Bridge to slow down Edgerton's pursuing troops, the fire was quickly put out. Edgerton followed Foster's men down through the Sparta area. The Union soldiers escaped across Otter's Creek and eventually returned to New Bern.

Tarboro was next occupied in the spring of 1864, by over 8,000 Confederate forces. General Hoke used Tarboro as the staging place for launching his campaign for the Battle of Plymouth on April 19, 1864. He had dozens of regiments sent to Tarboro by train, while others marched in. Hoke arranged his troops and gave marching orders from Tarboro. After the victorious campaign, the Confederate troops marched their 2,400 Union captives back to Tarboro They were held in a stockade built on the town common until they could be transported to Confederate prisons in western North Carolina and Georgia.

The heavy casualties caused the Female Academy to be turned into a second hospital. In his memoirs, Bishop Cheshire recorded that:

> each sick or wounded man was assigned to a family in town, some of the wealthiest families taking two; and the family, to which a man had been assigned, furnished, under the directions of the physicians in charge, such articles of food, clothing and bedding as the patient might require.

Cheshire also indicated that some of the wealthier families left Tarboro and moved to Louisburg or other piedmont communities to avoid the invading troops. He enumerated the changes in the county during the war years:

> Edgecombe was a rich and prosperous county of large plantations and many slaves. Cotton could no longer be gotten to market, and the fertile fields, formerly devoted to its culture, now yielded abundant crops of corn, peas, potatoes, and even oats and a little wheat. Chinese sugar cane, sorgum, was largely cultivated. Old looms and spinning wheels, and cotton cards were gotten out, and domestic manufactures of all kinds sprang up and supplied coarse but serviceable fabrics. Money sank lower and lower in value, and my father's salary began to be paid by supplies of corn, wood, and other such commodities. Meat became very scarce—but I do not remember that we were ever entirely without it, although from 1864 we had meat only at dinner, and then children were limited to one piece.

Civilians did what they could to live as normally as possible during the war years. Those who worked in Bellamy's Mill near Whitakers made caps for the Confederate Army. The Battle Mills in Rocky Mount produced uniform cloth before being destroyed in the raid of July 1863. The *Tarboro Southerner* continued to publish on a weekly basis, often reporting activities of troops and, when necessary, casualty records. One report in the summer of 1863 (before the Union raid) however, recounted a local accident. Colonel Martin and the 17th N.C. Regiment—which included Company I, the Edgecombe Rebels—were on a train between Tarboro and Rocky Mount when a broken axle derailed the train and destroyed several flat cars. The mail train from Tarboro arrived on the scene and transported the 20 wounded men to the Tarboro hospital.

Another unusual story involved a local family, but did not take place on a battlefield. Josiah Pender was a cousin of General Dorsey Pender and son of local merchant Solomon Pender. He operated a hotel in Beaufort at the beginning of the war, but when the Union occupied the coast, he lost his business. Pender then joined the Confederate Army and led the capture of Fort Macon. His wife died in the fall of 1861 and he went absent without leave; as a result, he was was dishonorably discharged from the army. He brought most of his nine children home to Tarboro to be looked after by relatives. He became reacquainted with a cousin, Laura Melvina Pender, and the couple married on September 23, 1862. Pender took his wife to Bermuda, where he was part of a blockade running operation, smuggling goods into the port of Wilmington for the Confederate cause.

Laura became pregnant and wanted to return to Tarboro to have her baby. Josiah first had to go to England for supplies, so he put Laura on a ship to Wilmington. Various versions of her story have been passed down through family lore and even published in United Daughters of the Confederacy articles. When her ship approached the Carolina coast, the Union ships attempted to capture it. The captain was ready to surrender until Mrs. Pender persuaded him—some say with a pistol—to break the blockade. The ship arrived safely in Wilmington and Laura took the train home to Tarboro. On October 19, 1863, she delivered her son, Josiah Keon Pender—named after his father and Governor Keon of Bermuda. Unfortunately, Josiah Pender contracted yellow fever and died at sea, never making it home to see his son.

AFTER THE WAR

Federal troops occupied Tarboro for a brief time in 1865 after the war ended. They established a camp across the river from town in an uninhabited area of bottom land (with fertile soil from the flooding river). As occurred in many places after the war, former slaves moved from their owner's plantations to open or unclaimed land to make a new start. Scores of former slaves moved to the low-lying area across the Tar River, where soldiers might provide supplies and protection. The new settlers named their community Freedom Hill or Liberty

Laura Melvina Pender was just 20 years old when the Civil War began. She married her widowed cousin Josiah Pender in the fall of 1862. He died at sea in 1864. Her portrait hangs in the Pender Museum, a part of the Blount-Bridgers House complex.

Hill, according to census records. By 1880, the community had a church, two grocery stores, and several school teachers—some sent in by the American Missionary Association. Two of the teachers, Robert Taylor and William Mabson, were elected to serve in the state legislature. In 1885, the community incorporated under the name Princeville—named for resident Turner Prince—becoming the first Black incorporated town in America.

After the war, both Tarboro and Rocky Mount grew, although the latter somewhat slowly. In 1860, Tarboro had a population of just over 1,000 and Rocky Mount about about 400. In 1867, Rocky Mount became incorporated with about 500 citizens. By 1870, Tarboro had over 1,300 residents equally divided between black and white. Edgecombe County grew to over 23,000, with almost two-thirds former slaves.

A report in the paper indicated that several land owners had sold their property to northern businessmen, while some lost their land at public auction. Others rented their land, while some continued to farm. The January 20, 1866 *Southerner* affirmed that "the cotton planters of Edgecombe have generally succeeded in hiring their freemen as laborers, for the cultivating of cotton for the present year. The usual wage is $13 per month and board." This was nearly what wages had been at the beginning of the war. The August 19, 1869 *Southerner* indicated that the cotton crop had recovered to its antebellum status:

After the Civil War, there was a need for public and private schools to educate African Americans. In 1895, Brick School opened as a private preparatory school in the northern corner of the county near Whitakers. Mr. Inborden was its principal.

> The cotton is magnificent, much of it as high as one's shoulders and such a display of squares of bolls as the oldest farmers has never seen before. We counted 150 and heard of 175 on a single stalk; most of the planters confidently expect a bale per acre and this is enough for anybody.

Just a decade later, another improvement in cotton made planting easier. Capt. T.M. Barna received a patent for the "Edgecombe Cotton Planter." The machine "made a public and critical exhibition" on Captain Dancy's "Model Farm," a test farm for experimenting with new products to improve farming. The planter was also exhibited at the North Carolina State Fair, where it won first prize. The March 20, 1879 *Southerner* boasted:

> The machine works easily, requiring not even a skilled plower. . . . The planter is light, is easily drawn by one horse, and the wheels are so adjusted that a man can sew his seed almost without touching the handles. . . . It is exceedingly substantial and well made.

Residents worked to rebuild the community after the war was over. New construction was all over town with "the spirit of improvement alive in our midst." The February 10, 1866 *Southerner* described the hectic activity:

> We have 14 Dry Goods Stores, 2 Drug Stores, 4 Groceries, 1 Hotel, 1 Livery Stable, 2 Shoe Shops, 2 Jewelry Stores, 5 Law Offices, 7 Doctors,

2 Millinery Establishments, 1 Bakery, 2 Tailor Shops, 1 Tin Shop, 1 Harness Shop, 2 Blacksmith Shops, 1 Coach Shop and 2 Express Company Offices, 1 Male and 2 Female Academies, 1 Photographic Gallery, and one Printing Press. But we are sorry to say we have no Mayor or Commissioners, and in consequence thereof our streets and bridges are in bad condition.

The 1867–1868 state business directory indicated that Edgecombe County had five private academies for whites and two public schools for freedmen. There were also 17 churches with two of them serving the black community. There was a new cabinet shop operated by John White. By 1869, the county had 8 lawyers, 24 physicians, and 12 mills. William Smith Battle rebuilt the burned mill in Rocky Mount, only to have it destroyed by arson in 1867. He rebuilt it yet again, to provide employment for his workers. Calvary Church, which had been started prior to the war, was completed and dedicated in 1867. That same year, the Agricultural Society reorganized and began publishing *The Reconstructed Farmer*, a journal to help farmers recover.

On May 16, 1867, freemen held a celebration in Tarboro. At least 2,500—including some from Martin and Pitt Counties—marched in the parade. According to a *Southerner* article:

Episcopalians established Calvary Parish in 1833. By the late 1850s, they needed a larger church and construction began in 1858 on a fine Gothic Revival structure designed by William Percival. The edifice was not completed until 1867, after the Civil War ended. Architecture historians describe this as one of the most important Gothic churches in the state.

77

The time was occupied by some of the lesser lights in speeches, which upon the whole, reflected much credit upon their sense of propriety, and what is demanded of them in their new relations. While some people indulged in rabid and mistaken notions of their newly acquired rights and privileges, the greater proportion gave good advice to their brethren, urging them to lay aside their present unfounded prejudices, and live on the best terms with their white neighbors.

Two of the speakers were James Harris and John O'Hara. Originally from the West Indies, O'Hara had studied law at Howard University and came to Tarboro as a missionary teacher. He was elected to the North Carolina Assembly in 1868 and to Congress from the North Carolina Second District in 1882. Several local men, including some former slaves, became active in county and state government. Henry Cherry, a former slave, was elected to the state convention in 1868 to draw up a new state constitution. He also served as a county commissioner before being elected to the North Carolina Senate in 1868 and the North Carolina General Assembly in 1884. Cherry had two daughters who married political leaders in the state. His daughter Cora married George White, while his daughter Louise married Henry Cheatham. Both of these men went on

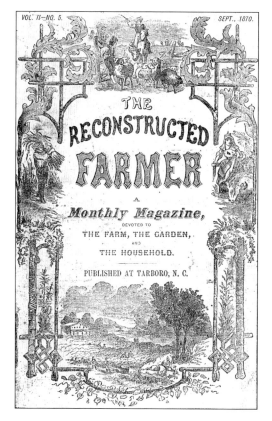

Edgecombe County continued to be a leader in agriculture in the state even after the war. The Reconstructed Farmer *was a monthly magazine produced in Tarboro with advice on farm techniques to improve crop yield. This magazine was a forerunner of* The Progressive Farmer. *(Courtesy of Edgecombe County Memorial Library.)*

Dred Wimberly was a slave belonging to the Battle family before the Civil War. After the war, he was elected to the North Carolina General Assembly and later to the North Carolina Senate. (Courtesy of North Carolina Office of Archives and History.)

to be elected to the U.S. Congress representing the North Carolina Second District. Cherry was a well-respected man in the community. He died of typhoid fever in the summer of 1885. The July 16, 1885 *Southerner* eulogized him:

> Though a colored man Henry Cherry commanded the confidence and respect of both races. He was honest, straightforward and lacking in the bitterness that marks the course of so many politicians. He also had the position of town commissioner for several terms and township constable. His funeral on Sunday was largely attended by the citizens and the Fulton Fire Company of which he was a member.

Between 1868 and 1900, over three dozen African Americans served in the local or state government. Born a slave to the James S. Battle family in 1848, Dred Wimberly agreed to work for the Battles after the war. He became an overseer for his former owner, Kemp Plummer Battle, who had married James Battle's daughter Patty. Wimberly was elected to the North Carolina General Assembly in 1879 and ten years later to the state senate. After that, he went to Washington as a civil servant in Congress. He married twice and fathered a total of 18 children. A state historic marker designates his home, which is still standing on Raleigh Street across from Pineview Cemetery in Rocky Mount. Wimberly died in 1937 and is buried in Unity Cemetery.

John C. Dancy was also a former slave, although he was just eight years old when the Civil War ended. He attended Howard University and became active in the Republican party. He was elected the local register of deeds and served as editor of the A.M.E. Zion newspaper. He was appointed customs collector in Wilmington. (Courtesy of North Carolina Office of Archives and History.)

Another political activist was John C. Dancy, the son of an Edgecombe County slave. Dancy was educated at Howard University and became an early principal and teacher in Tarboro. He served county and state offices before federal appointments as a customs agent in Wilmington and recorder of deeds in Washington, D.C. Locally, Dancy was president of a temperance convention, secretary of the North Carolina Republican Conventions in the 1880s, and register of deeds for Edgecombe County in 1880 and 1882. He was also editor of the *Star of Zion*, a newsletter for the A.M.E. Church.

African-American churches had a steady growth in the last quarter of the nineteenth century. St. Paul's Baptist Church was established in 1872. St. Luke's Episcopal Church was formed in 1870 by the African-American communicants of Calvary. They worshiped in the old Calvary building until their new church was dedicated on the corner of Pitt and Panola Streets in 1885. The first minister of St. Luke's was the Reverend Doctor John William Perry, a recent graduate of St. Augustine College in Raleigh. Dr. Perry also served as the headmaster of St.

Luke's Parochial School, situated next to the church, from 1881 to 1918. His daughter Catherine and her husband, the Reverend Milton M. Weston, assumed leadership of the school for the next several years. Other African-American churches were A.M.E. Zion in Princeville in 1866, Red Hill near Whitakers in 1875, and the Bethlehem Missionary Baptist Church in Leggett in 1879.

A new denomination appeared in Tarboro in 1872, when the Presbyterian church was established on the corner of St. James and St. Patrick Streets on the edge of the Old Town Cemetery. Tradition refers to this congregation as "the church of the three Annas," after the wives of three staunch Presbyterian community leaders who were named Anna (Mrs. George Howard, Mrs. Augustus Harvey MacNair, and Mrs. Frank Wilkinson) and who wanted a church of their denomination. In the early 1900s, the original structure was sold to Eastern Star Baptist Church and moved across town to a new location on east Church Street. A new brick church with classical and Romanesque elements was constructed in 1908 and christened Howard Memorial Presbyterian Church.

As Edgecombe farmers recovered from the war, their production of cotton and other crops increased river traffic. In 1867, the steamer *Cotton Plant* began a regular route up the Tar River to Tarboro from Washington. Three days a week, it brought fresh fish up from the coast and transported cotton downriver. The ship sank in the fall of 1869 in the Tar River near Greenville, but the crew fortunately managed to save the cargo. The steamer was eventually recovered and repaired, and by summer of the next year, returned to her route for many years. The *Cotton*

Batts Chapel Baptist Church was one of the first African-American churches in the county. It opened in 1851. (Courtesy of North Carolina Office of Archives and History.)

Plant was soon joined by the *Vesta*, "the largest, finest, and most commodious boat that has ever reached here," according to the November 2, 1871 *Southerner*. Other steamers that cruised the Tar River included the *Isis*, *North East*, *Greenville*, and *Edgecombe*—the last owned by the Clyde Line of Washington, North Carolina. In 1879, the *R.L. Myers* was launched from Washington, North Carolina. The ship had a 40-horsepower engine capable of maintaining 8 miles per hour, the capacity for 400 cotton bales, and 3 saloons for passenger travel. The ships on the Tar River brought fresh seafood upriver, leading the newspaper in the fall of 1873 to advertise five different oyster bars on Main Street in Tarboro.

River travel was perhaps the quickest way to get to Greenville and Washington in the last quarter of the nineteenth century. While stage lines continued to serve some parts of the county, especially on the eastern roads of the county, the railroad was the most effective means of transportation if going west to Rocky Mount or Raleigh or even north to Virginia. Sometimes though, river travel took unexpected turns. The December 19, 1872 *Southerner* reported the story of a wholesale merchant representing a branch from a New York firm who traveled downriver towards Washington. As the *Vesta* approached Greenville,

> A Negro man fell overboard. The steamer immediately slowed and a
> small boat lowered, but such was the speed that the unfortunate man

George Matthewson, a free black carpenter, built this cottage on the corner of Church and Panola Streets in the early 1860s. In addition to the detailed sawn-work columns, the house also had a cistern and indoor running water.

must have perished but the gallant conduct of the gentleman. Seeing the danger, he threw off his coat and boots, spring in the water and succeeded in reaching the drowning man as he was going down for the third time. They were both taken in by the small boat, but the gentleman is said to have presented a laughable appearance upon his arrival at Washington. Being a rather lengthy individual the pants he borrowed from some short friend on the boat did not add much dignity to his general bearing.

The newspaper identified the merchant as Samuel S. Nash, a 24-year-old wholesale grocery dealer and cotton buyer representing the Houses of William and Murchison of Wilmington and New York. He had joined the Confederate Army at age 15 and served in the 55th North Carolina Regiment until being captured near Appomattox. After the war, he came to Tarboro as a merchant. For many years he ran S.S. Nash & Company, a hardware and wholesale store. In the 1890s, he became a cotton buyer. In 1910, he managed Edgecombe Homestead Savings and Loan, a business that lasted for over 80 years. Nash spent 40 years serving three of the mission churches of Calvary Episcopal Church: St. Mary's at Speed, Grace at Lawrence, and St. Matthew's. Nash married Annie Gray Cheshire, daughter of the rector of Calvary, and the couple bore six children. A member of the Lewis-Dowd-Wyatt Camp of the Confederate Veterans, Nash attended the veterans reunions until his death in 1930. The county lost "The Grand Old Man of Edgecombe" at the age of 81.

After the war, immigrants came to Edgecombe County from various parts of Europe. One group of 28 Swiss arrived in 1869. Most worked on the farms of John Staton, J.W. Pippin, William Pippen, and Mrs. Ed Foxhall. At least one family, the Demuths, settled in the Crisp area and are buried in a cemetery behind the Eagles store. Fred Demuth worked on the Cotton Valley plantation and sold ice cut from farm ponds. Another Swiss family lived in the Hart Mill area and sold locally-made Swiss cheese. Others are reported by the 1870 census as butchers or saloon keepers in Rocky Mount. One family was employed by the Zoellers in Tarboro. The Zoellers had immigrated from Bavaria, Germany in the 1850s. Edward Zoeller was a fresco painter whose work still survives in several area homes. One of his sons operated a stationery store after the war, which merged with Dr. L.L. Staton to become Staton and Zoeller Drug Store.

An 1871 political change produced long-term economic effects on Edgecombe County. One version of the story said that there was a disagreement between Nash and Edgecombe Counties regarding the maintenance of the bridge over the Tar River in Rocky Mount, which marked the county line. Repeated repair requests from Nash officials went unanswered, so Nash County took over the bridge and gained permission from the state to extend the county line. Another story said that Edgecombe County wanted to balance its population and willingly gave up part of Rocky Mount so that some of the African Americans would be in Nash County. Examination of various records makes two points clear. First,

Rocky Mount had incorporated in 1867 and was a growing town located in Edgecombe County. Once the county line moved, Nash County expanded its tax base by including the largest business in the town, Battle Cotton Mills (later Rocky Mount Mills). Second, the moving of the county line did not follow procedure. New bills were to be proposed in the general assembly and presented in both counties for local approval. However, the bill that changed the Nash and Edgecombe County line was introduced and passed despite protests and petitions from Edgecombe County. The outcome was that Whitakers, Battleboro, Rocky Mount, and Sharpsburg—all originally in Edgecombe County—were divided between the two counties with the Wilmington to Weldon Railroad as the new county line. Nash County was ordered to pay $800 for the approximately 1-mile-wide and 18-miles-long 11,500 acres it gained.

This loss was offset by several new businesses that opened in the 1870s and added to the economic growth of Edgecombe County. W.S. Clark & Sons began supplying farmers with seeds and farm tools in 1872. That same year, A.J. Hines also began the Edgecombe Agricultural Works in Tarboro. In Rocky Mount, Walker Henderson made and sold barrels. After years of advertising as a furniture dealer and casket maker, Carlisle Funeral Home opened in 1874 and is still in business over 125 years later. In 1877, competing merchant J.E. Simmons also advertised as a cabinet maker and undertaker. Today, that business is operated by the fourth generation of the Simmons family as J.E. Simmons Furniture Company. Tarboro also had three hotels, two jewelers, a baker, five dress makers, two book and stationary stores, an auction house, and numerous grocery and general stores. Staton and Zoeller opened a drug store and sold their own "Edgecombe Fair" Cologne. Sparta boasted a whiskey distillery, a liquor store, a miller, two grocers, three general stores, and one saloon. Whitakers also had several general stores and the only bowling saloon in the county. John Portis had a shoe factory in Battleboro. W.E. Fountain came to Tarboro from Rocky Mount in the 1870s to be the first telegraph operator in Edgecombe County. In 1878, Tarboro expanded Main Street from the town common north to the railroad depot. The next year, two baseball grounds were created on the common.

Edgecombe County lost one of its respected citizens in April 1874 when Dr. James J. Philips died at his home, Mount Moriah. Philip's grandfather had migrated from Virginia in the early 1700s, one of the first settlers in the northern part of the county. Philips was born in 1798 and studied medicine under Dr. Cullen Battle before going to Philadelphia for additional training. He returned to North Carolina and practiced medicine in a five-county area, eventually becoming an honorary member of the Medical Society of North Carolina. Dr. Philips was known for his fine medical care and considered by many to be one of the best physicians in the state, and he was a farmer as well. Philips was a member of the Edgecombe Agricultural Society and lectured that group on new farming practices that would improve the soil and apply scientific techniques to crops.

A part of the 1868 revised North Carolina Constitution reorganized local government and created townships in each county. Prior to the constitutional change, the area had 20 districts, each named for the recorder who collected taxes or votes. After each township elected representatives to the new county government, insuring a more democratic local government. Today these 14 townships still exist, but changes in local government form small elective districts for the commissioners. The townships were Tarboro Lower Conetoe, Upper Conetoe, Deep Creek, Lower Fishing Creek, Upper Fishing Creek, Swift Creek, Sparta, Otters Creek, Lower Town Creek, Upper Town Creek, Walnut Creek, Rocky Mount, and Cokey. The county commissioners elected in 1878, after the end of military occupation and Reconstruction, included three African Americans: Frank Dancy, Frank Whitted, and Clinton Battle. The other commissioners were John Lancaster and N.B. Bellamy. This ratio represented the population of the county: 15,112 African Americans and 7,858 whites.

Students stand in front of the new Bellamy School located in township number six, Upper Fishing Creek. (Courtesy of North Carolina Office of Archives and History.)

4. PROGRESS AND CHANGE 1880–1920

In the last two decades of the nineteenth century, Edgecombe County continued to prosper in agriculture. The increasing population led to the development of more schools and churches and the publication of six newspapers. Immigrants opened businesses and created new communities with interesting cultural traditions. The 1880 population was over 26,100—an increase of over 3,000 from the previous census. Tarboro saw an increase from 1,300 in 1870 to over 1,600 in 1880. Rocky Mount, which was now divided between two counties, had a population increase of about 120, but it is not clear how much of that was in Edgecombe County.

The winter of 1880 and 1881 provided record-breaking weather. The paper reported extremely cold conditions from Maine to Mexico, with snow storms, hail, and severe temperatures. Tarboro usually sees only a quick snowfall once every five to six years, but by January 6, 1881, the community had enjoyed five consecutive days of ice skating on the area ponds. People converted buggies to sleighs by replacing the wheels with homemade runners. Judge Howard, perhaps the wealthiest man in town, delivered many free wagon loads of wood to the elderly and the poor to prevent their suffering.

"No town in the State has superior railroad and navigation facilities. Four lines of railroads and three steamboat lines give to Tarboro all the benefits and advantages of cheap freights and easy communication with all sections" claimed the 1891 promotional tract *Edgecombe County North Carolina: Her People and Resources. The Foremost Agricultural Section of the State.* The Tar River and the railroad continued to be the most common means of transporting goods to regional markets. The railroad line was extended from Tarboro to Williamston in 1882, connecting the southeastern part of the county to the county seat.

High yields of cotton continued to be transported downriver to Greenville and Washington. The *Cotton Plant*, a popular steamer that had been on the river since the 1860s, caught fire in December 1890. Area fire departments managed to save some of the cargo, but the craft was lost. Several new steamers appeared on the river, but some had problems with the bridges. When the river was high, the larger

The Tar River was the major route used by farmers and merchants to transport goods downriver to other markets and ports and to import goods from other cities. This paddlewheel steamboat, Tarboro, *is approaching the steamboat landing. (Courtesy of Edgecombe County Memorial Library.)*

boats could not navigate upstream because of the low bridges at Sparta. In 1881, the *Tarboro* was added to the Tar River fleet. She was the lightest draught vessel on the river, usually taking on 3 inches of water when empty and no more than 10 inches when fully loaded. Captain Mayo announced that the steamer *Greenville* was available for transport in 1885. By 1889, the *Beta* operated north of Tarboro to Shiloh Mills until it hit a bridge in 1892. The accident resulted in a drawbridge replacing the former structure to allow for easier river navigation. The last steamer introduced to the Tar River was the second *Tarboro*, on December 1, 1898. Just five years later, the lack of river improvements and the competition of the railroads caused Old Dominion Steamship Company to announce that it was taking all of its boats off the river. Only those of the Tar River Oil Company were left in operation.

Existing business communities were Tarboro, Battleboro, Hartsboro, Old Sparta, Rocky Mount, and Whitakers. Battleboro had a dozen general stores, four blacksmiths, and a livery stable. The oldest settlement in the county, Sparta, was renamed Old Sparta in 1881 by the U.S. Post Office, when a community in the western part of the state also used the name Sparta. The town of Old Sparta had eight general stores, three liquor stores, two nurseries, a saloon, and a mill in 1890. Hartsboro was a settlement in western Edgecombe County between Tarboro and

Many former slaves from Tarboro moved across the Tar River to a low-lying area and created the community of Liberty Hill in the 1870s. Turner Prince was one of the earliest land owners and this is his house in what became Princeville. In 1885, Princeville was the first incorporated African-American town in the United States. (Courtesy of North Carolina Office of Archives and History.)

Rocky Mount with one general store; today the area is known as Hartsease. A new community in the southeast, Conetoe, began as a post office in 1883 and by 1890 had three grocery stores and five general stores. Other communities that were too small to be considered towns included Coakley, Doehead, Hickory Hill, Kingsboro, Lawrence, Mildred, St. Lewis, and Wrendale.

Princeville, incorporated in 1885 as the first town chartered by African Americans, did not have a separate post office, but did have a separate town government. The community experienced its first flood in 1889, but the impact was not serious enough to cause the residents to leave the area. The town opened a public school in 1883. The first church in the community, Mt. Zion Primitive Baptist Church, opened in 1871. It was soon joined by Macedonia Baptist Church, the A.M.E. Zion Church, and St. John's Missionary Baptist Church. By the end of the century, Princeville boasted ten grocery stores, a restaurant, a butcher shop, and a jeweler. Mayors included M.S. Dancy in 1890 and H.N. Cherry from 1896 to 1897. Robert Taylor, a Jamaican, came to the area in the late 1860s as a school teacher. He was active in local politics and served as a Tarboro commissioner in 1890.

THE JEWISH COMMUNITY

Part of the growth of the area, especially in Tarboro, can be attributed to the increase in German and Jewish immigration. Prior to 1860, there were only two German families. The Zoellers had migrated from Bavaria in 1852 and were well-established in the community by the 1880s. Jacob Feldenheimer and his brother Joseph arrived shortly before the Civil War from Wurtenberg and opened a store, while Jacob's wife Rachel operated a millinery shop downtown. The Feldenheimer family was Jewish and had connections with other Jewish families in Richmond, Virginia. By 1870, the Baers and Joels from Prussia, the Heilbroners and Sorgs from Bavaria, and the Odenheimers from Baden were among the many Jewish immigrants that settled in Edgecombe County. Most set up a shop or general store. The Congregation B'nai Israel first met in 1877 and continued into the next century. Combined with the Swiss, who were living on farms, there were over 35 immigrant families living in the county.

Between 1880 and 1900, another 50 families moved into the county. In this second wave were families from Russia, Poland, Holland, and Germany. Most of these were Jewish merchants who operated clothing and mercantile businesses along Main Street. In fact, one newspaper article in the 1870s referred to two

Between 1885 and 1915, Tarboro expanded north and featured numerous Victorian homes along Main Street. The Lichenstein-Alley House, noted for its horseshoe-shaped entry, was built in the 1890s by a German immigrant family, the Lichensteins. S.R. Alley purchased the house in the early 1900s for his second wife. He later moved to Wilson, North Carolina and sold this house to the Boykin family.

blocks of Main Street as "Little Jerusalem." Ads in the area papers reminded customers when the stores would be closed for special Jewish holidays. Although there was an independent congregation in Tarboro, connections were maintained with Richmond. When one of the local residents died, the family sent the remains to Richmond or to Goldsboro, a town about 50 miles south of Tarboro, for burial in blessed ground.

By 1880, there were approximately 100 faithful Jewish worshippers in the area. Then a second group of immigrants, numbering about two dozen families (many of whom were related to each other) arrived. This group was Orthodox and, unlike the earlier German-speaking wave, spoke Hebrew and Yiddish. This second group, also unlike in Richmond and other Southern towns, merged with the first and the synagogue became reformed. Families included the Lichtensteins, Shugars, Rosenblooms, Rosenbaums, Meyers, Kaufmans, Cohens, Whitlocks, Kreslowskis, and Adlers. Family units often included a brother or sister or in-law. A brother might marry and bring his wife's family to this area, or similarly, a young woman might marry and bring her husband to work in her

By the 1890s, Tarboro had a sizable Jewish population. Immigrants came into the area from parts of Germany and Russia beginning in the 1860s. A synagogue was completed in 1897 and was torn down in the 1970s when the congregation disbanded. One of its original windows was saved and installed in the chapel at the Fountains of the Albemarle retirement community.

family's business. An 1869 wedding was described in detail in the paper as "interesting Hebrew nuptial rites." To aid the many local guests, the Rabbi from Richmond conducted most of the service in English.

Jewish residents opened a variety of businesses in town, many of which continued to operate until the late twentieth century. Jews managed a hotel and the opera house. Henry Weber, a baker from Bavaria, opened an ice cream saloon in 1881. By 1890, an orthodox congregation was established along with several community societies, such as a men's lodge and a literary society in Tarboro. Many Jews were also active in non-denominational organizations, such as the Masons and the local militia band. Henry Morris was elected mayor of Tarboro in 1885. The *Carolina Banner*, reported on a Jewish Ball in 1889:

> As was announced last week our Hebrew populace gave a grand ball and supper Tuesday evening Jan. 29th. They never do things by halves and this occasion was no exception to the general rule.
>
> The ladies were all handsomely and tastily attired and many were the diamonds sparking here and there under the brilliant rays of the gas. The gentlemen wore the regulation evening dress suits.
>
> Dancing began at 10 p.m. and lasted until 3 a.m. At 11:30 o'clock supper was announced and the participants in the ball—50 in number— proceed to Cooper's café where there awaited them a most handsome supper, such as only Cooper can prepare and at 12:30 they again returned to the ball-room to finish their evening's enjoyment. Music for the evening was furnished by the colored string band.

The young Jewish people formed the Aguilar Literary Circle in 1894, meeting on a weekly basis to discuss recent works and debate current issues. They read the works of their namesake, poet Grace Aguilar, and other popular writers including Charles Dickens. They debated topics such as the contributions of immigrants to the United States, the benefits of Reformed Judaism, capital punishment, and women's suffrage.

By 1900, many of the early Jewish immigrants and several of the second group built beautiful Victorian mansions along north Main Street, demonstrating that they were a part of the financial elite of the town. The synagogue, constructed in 1895, resembled a traditional southern church with a steeple and stained glass windows. While keeping their faith, the Jews had otherwise merged with the Southern town.

A smaller, third Jewish migration occurred during World War I, but by 1920, most of the original Jewish settlers were gone—either having died or moved. Some, like the Feildenheimers, went back to Richmond. Others, like the Whitlocks, moved west to areas such as Asheville. The second and third generations often converted to other religions, although only once did a Gentile convert to Judaism. Miss Addie Jenkins converted to Judaism and changed her name to Sarah when she married Julius Rosenbaum in 1891. By 1950, the B'nai

Israel Synagogue was no longer active, its members having moved to the larger Temple Beth El in nearby Rocky Mount.

OUTSTANDING CITIZENS

One member of the Jewish population of Tarboro became a successful historian. Gaston Lichtenstein was born in Tarboro in 1879 to David and Hannah Zander Lichtenstein. He attended the Tarboro Male Academy under the direction of Frank Wilkinson and graduated from both the Hebrew Union College in Cinicinnati (with a Bachelor in Hebrew Letters) in 1899 and the University of Cincinnati in 1900. He became a prominent historian fluent in seven languages and a member of the American Historical Association. After moving to Richmond, Virginia, he produced a major history of Patrick Henry and another of the Jews in Richmond. Because his roots were in Edgecombe County, he often submitted local history columns to the newspaper and published several monographs on Tarboro and Edgecombe County history. He died on January 16, 1954 and his obituary appeared in the *New York Times.*

Another noted Tarboro resident and a contemporary of Gaston Lichtenstein was John Spencer Bassett. A state historical marker on the corner of Albemarle Avenue and Wilson Street marks the location of his home and his accomplishments as: "Professor at Trinity College, 1894–1906 and Secretary, American Historical Association, 1919–1928 born here." The sign doesn't say John was the son of a building contractor. He graduated from Trinity College in 1888 and became an English professor there. He continued his education at Johns Hopkins where he earned a Ph.D. in history. He returned to Trinity (soon to be Duke University) and taught history and English for several years while publishing essays on North Carolina, Southern, and African-American history. Bassett's work drew the wrath of Raleigh editor Josephus Daniels, who demanded Bassett be fired. Bassett offered to resign to avoid controversy at the college, but the school refused his resignation and the students petitioned to keep him. Eventually, he moved on to Smith College in Massachusetts, and founded the *South Atlantic Quarterly*. He was one of the founders of the American Historical Association. He was killed by a car accident in Washington, D.C. in 1928.

In the last two decades of the nineteenth century, Edgecombe County lost several leading citizens who had been instrumental in building the agricultural, economic, and political facets of the county. John L. Bridgers died in 1884 and his brother Robert in 1888. Cabinetmaker and business man Francis Bond passed on in 1890. In 1899, Joseph Blount Cheshire, rector at Calvary Church for 50 years, died, followed in 1900 by Elias Carr, an agricultural leader and former North Carolina governor.

John Luther Bridgers was remembered by many for his military service in the Edgecombe Guards during the Civil War. Bridgers was also an active business leader and progressive farmer before the war. A graduate of the University of North Carolina, Bridgers returned to his native Edgecombe County to practice

Rebecca Dicken married John Luther Bridgers in 1847. In 1850, they moved into the Grove, the former home of Thomas Blount. The Bridgers remodeled the home by adding the wrap-around porch. Rebecca died in 1865. Her portrait hangs in the Blount-Bridgers House.

law. He was a director for the Tarboro branch of the state bank, and a member of the local and state agricultural societies. Bridgers often competed with his brother Robert in using scientific farming to improve crop production. He was also supportive of the construction of the new Calvary Episcopal Church. Bridgers had a son and daughter by his first wife, Rebecca Dicken, before she died in 1865. He then married Mary Elizabeth Battle and had four more children. His two daughters, Loulie and Mary, became school teachers; Bridgers School on the eastern edge of the town common was named for them. John is buried with both his wives and most of his children in Calvary Churchyard.

R.R. Bridgers was often overlooked because of the influence of his brother John Luther Bridgers, a Civil War veteran, and his nephew Henry Clark Bridgers, who founded the East Carolina Railway. His obituary from the December 13, 1888 *Southerner* was a tribute to the man:

> Robert Rufus Bridgers was stricken dead with apoplexy while addressing the Ways and Means Committee of the South Carolina legislature in Columbia at 7 o'clock Monday evening. Bridgers was born

in this county Nov. 28th, 1819 making him sixty-nine years old last month. As a boy he was studious, steady and obedient, but his chief characteristic was his parental dutifulness and tenderness which abided undimmed until the death of his mother a few years since. He graduated from the State university [University of North Carolina] with first distinction in 1841 and was at once licensed to practice law where he met with success from the beginning. In 1844 he was elected to the lower house of the legislature, the youngest member in that body and served in the judiciary committee. Abandoning politics he gave his entire attention to the law and farming. While he was a leading practitioner, he became one of the foremost planters in the county and the largest cotton producer in the state. He was tendered the Attorney Generalship of the state and the position of Circuit Judge, both of which he declined.

In 1851 he became president of the Tarboro Branch Bank and in 1856 he was again returned to the legislature of which he remained a member until 1861 as the leader of the House and chairman of the Judiciary Committee. Upon the organization of the Confederate Congress, he was elected from this district and continued as a member until its desolution. In that body he served as a member of the Military and the Special Finance Committees.

When the war ended Bridgers was elected president of the W[ilmington] & W[eldon] railroad which he saved from the wreck that engulfed all the state roads by his enlightened management and tireless energy. He bears the proud and peerless records of being elected President 21 times of the W&W Railroad. When he died he was president of the W&W, C&A [sic A&C, Atlantic & Carolina] and A[berdeen] & R[ockfish] Railroads. In 1868, the cooperation of a few Baltimore capitalists was secured by him, resulting in the establishment of the Atlantic Coastline.

Bridgers was well known to every man middle age and older in this county and section and he leaves a widow, a number of children and a large number of sorrowing relatives. He removed from Tarboro to Wilmington when he became president of the W&W railroad and has since resided there. In addition to the railroad duties he was President of Navassa Guano Company of Wilmington whose affairs he managed with consummate ability.

In late August 1890, Tarboro experienced a mystery that ended in tragedy. Frank Bond had inherited his father's furniture factory in the 1850s and acquired several lots in town during his years in business. The 70-year-old craftsman and businessman disappeared from his home in the middle of the night. The August 28 paper announced a reward and many townspeople searched for the missing man. According to the paper, "for sometime he was not been in normal health."

He had recently lost a dear friend, Mr. Robert Austin, and was depressed over the demolition of some buildings in town. The river was searched to no avail after reports of an unexplained "splash" on the night he disappeared. Three days later, his body was discovered approximately 10 miles from Washington by one of the steamers that traveled the river. The body was returned to Tarboro. Because of the unusual circumstances surrounding his death—was it suicide or had he fallen into the river in the night?—there was some disagreement over his funeral. Nevertheless, services were held the same evening:

> By a large concourse it [his coffin] was followed to the Episcopal Church, where the appropriate services were held, then to the old cemetery where he had a plot.
>
> The scene here was solemn and impressive. Night had fallen. As the funeral cortege reached the burial ground, the moon rose large and full of splendor, throwing dense shadows in the "City of the Dead." By the light of a lamp, the venerable man of God, J.B. Cheshire, D.D. conducted the brief services. The stillness was solemn, broken only by

Lewis Bond operated a furniture factory in Tarboro from the 1820s until he retired in the 1840s. His son Francis carried on the factory until the late 1880s, making a variety of furniture including cabinets, sideboards, bedsteads, tables, wardrobes, and bureaus—such as this one dated about 1840. This gentleman's bureau has a fold-down panel that reveals a desktop.

Bracebridge Hall, c. 1825, located in the Old Sparta community, was the home of the Jonas Johnston Carr family. His son, Elias Carr, developed this into an outstanding plantation. (Courtesy of North Carolina Office of Archives and History.)

      the earnest utterances of the minister and the hoot of the bird of the night, an owl.

Bond died with no children. He did leave a lot on the corner of Pitt and Main Streets for building a new Masonic lodge, which was constructed later. He also left money to the ministers of Calvary Episcopal and St. Luke's Episcopal churches.

The Reverend Dr. Joseph Blount Cheshire, who conducted the service for Mr. Bond, had been baptizing, marrying, and burying people in Tarboro since 1842. A native of Edenton, he studied law in Raleigh. He was ordained in Christ Church in Raleigh in 1840. The next year, he began ministering in Scotland Neck and helped establish Trinity Church, serving as rector there for 25 years. He became the rector of Calvary in Tarboro in 1842 and served both churches until he resigned from Trinity in 1869. A strong interest in botany led to his beautifying the grounds around Calvary with unusual plants not native to the area. During the Civil War, he ministered to the wounded at the hospitals and held funerals for those that didn't survive. He also financed the printing of the *Prayer Book of the Confederate States*, which was a modification of the *Book of Common Prayer.*

Reverend Cheshire conducted services for black parishioners each Sunday. His son remembered that before and during the war, African Americans were welcomed at the regular morning services, but had to sit in the balcony. During the afternoon services, Blacks sat in the regular pews and any Whites who attended had to sit in the balcony. Cheshire supported the 1867 development of St. Augustine's College in Raleigh, a private Episcopal school to train Black ministers and teachers. He also helped establish St. Luke's as the first African-American parish in the Diocese of North Carolina in 1870.

Cheshire's last service as minister was the funeral of his wife in 1893. He had married Elizabeth Toole Parker in 1843. She was the daughter of Theophilus Parker, the Senior Warden at Calvary and the brother of Frances Parker. The couple had four children: son Joseph Blount Cheshire Jr., who became a minister like his father; son Theophilus; daughter Annie Gray, who married Samuel Nash; and daughter Katherine. Cheshire died September 9, 1899 and was buried in his beloved churchyard. His son, the Right Reverend Joseph Blount Cheshire Jr., became Bishop of the North Carolina Diocese in 1893.

Edgecombe County continued to be represented in state and national politics. Elias Carr from Old Sparta became governor in 1892. From 1897 to 1901, George White of Tarboro was be the last Black congressman from the South to serve in the House of Representatives until just before World War II. Elias Carr was born on February 25, 1839 to Jonas Johnston Carr and Elizabeth Jane Hilliard at Bracebridge Hall in southern Edgecombe County near Sparta. His fraternal great-grandfather was Colonel Jonas Johnston, who served in the American Revolution. His mother's family was among the earliest settlers of Nash County. Bracebridge Hall had been completed in two years as the center of a 2,000-acre farm now known as the Carr farm. Both of Carr's parents died before he was five years old, and he was reared by an uncle in Warren County. He attended the W.J. Bingham School at the Oaks in Orange County. He spent two years at the University of North Carolina and graduated from the University of Virginia.

In May 1859, Carr married Eleanor Kearney, a neighbor from Warren County. They bought out his brother's share and made Bracebridge Hall their home. In September 1861, Carr enlisted as a private in Company G, 41st Regiment of the Third Calvary. When this first enlistment was up, he returned home to run his farm, but was called back into service before the Civil War was over and obtained the rank of colonel. After the war, Carr returned to his home and dedicated himself to his family and to the establishment of an extraordinary plantation.

Carr became active in community affairs. He was on the school board in 1869 for the Sparta district; then served for 15 years as an Edgecombe County commissioner. He founded and was the first president of the North Carolina Society of the Sons of the Revolution, while his wife Eleanor was a charter member of the North Carolina Daughters of the American Revolution. He was also a stock holder and member of the board of directors of Rocky Mount Mills. The Carrs attended Calvary Church, but Mrs. Carr also attended her home Methodist church when summering in Warrenton.

Carr's first interest was always agriculture. He used scientific methods and emphasized diversification. He grew cotton and tobacco along with corn, peas, and peanuts. He also raised dairy cows and sold both milk and butter. He grew fruits and vegetables for home use. He educated farmers in the building of silos and sold bricks and lumber from his farm. He kept detailed records which he used to help with future crops. Carr also served as the North Carolina delegate to the National Farmer's Congress in 1886. He was the first president of the Farmer's Institute of Edgecombe County and the first president of the North Carolina Farmer's Association in 1887. Carr desired an agricultural college for the state and once the North Carolina Agricultural and Mechanical College (now North Carolina State University) was established in 1889, he served on its board of trustees.

Carr's agricultural interests led to his being recognized by area politicians. During the 1890s, dissatisfaction with the two major political parties caused farmers and working class citizens to form the Populist movement. To counteract this new party, the state Democratic party wanted a gubernatorial candidate that would also appeal to the Populists, and Carr was that person. A January 1893 *Southerner* reported:

> Colonel Carr is nominated on the sixth ballot at the Democratic convention. Local citizens planned a rousing reception for his return

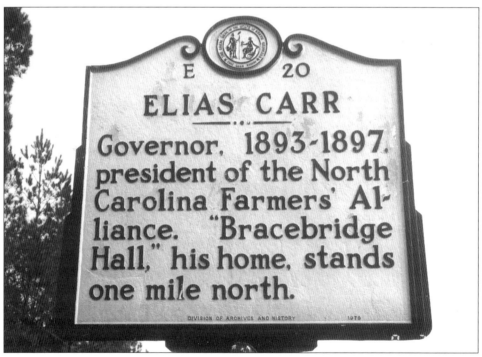

In the fall of 1892, Edgecombe citizens were celebrating the election of Elias Carr—from the Old Sparta community—as governor of North Carolina. Carr was known throughout the state for the diversified farming techniques at his home Bracebridge, which he had built up to one of the finest farms in the state after the Civil War.

Even with the Civil War over, the Edgecombe Guards continued to meet and train as the local militia. Carl William Jeffreys was captain of the Guards in the late 1870s and early 1880s. Jeffreys was also captain of Company I in the North Carolina Second Regiment in the Spanish American War, and later became general manager of the Tarboro Knitting Mills. (Courtesy of North Carolina Office of Archives and History.)

from Raleigh. The town was agog with joy and enthusiasm. It is reported that Mayor Fountain danced in the street and that the Methodists will not even discipline him.

Elias Carr became the second Edgecombe County native to serve as governor of the state. He was inaugurated in January 1893, leaving Tarboro on a special train to Raleigh. According to the paper, he had a big send off by the local militia Edgecombe Guards and numerous Tarboro citizens. He was met in Raleigh by the governor's guards and a reception committee. After the inauguration and a two-hour reception, the Carrs hosted an inaugural ball.

Turner and Bridger's biography describes Elias Carr as living "the life of a country gentleman, and Bracebridge Hall epitomized Southern hospitality. . . . He was a modest, unassuming, typical gentleman . . . a man with positive convictions and of clean character." Carr served one term as governor, focusing on the development of public schools and colleges, road improvement, and prison facilities. When his term ended in 1897, he retired to his plantation and died just three years later. Carr was 61 years old and left a wife and five children. His obituary in the July 26, 1900 *Southerner* reported the following:

Another important election occurred in 1898, when George Henry White was elected to represent the Second North Carolina District in the United States Congress. White, a former teacher and lawyer from New Bern, moved to Tarboro after marrying Cora Cherry. Despite a white supremacist movement, White was elected and served until 1901. (Courtesy of North Carolina Office of Archives and History.)

To all trusts he was faithful; as a neighbor he was among the best; as a host he dispensed a hospitality bounteous and cordial, and with a tact is scarcely equaled. . . . As governor he was the same unostentatious gentleman that presided over his farm to which he returned after his public service. He devoted himself to the welfare of the citizens of the state. When he died a vast concourse of friends from all parts of the county came to testify and esteem a respect for a man whose private and public life met their approval.

Another significant politician from Edgecombe County was George Henry White, an African American elected to congress from the North Carolina Second District. Originally from Bladen County, White was principal of the State Normal School in New Bern. He married Cora Cherry, daughter of Henry Cherry of Tarboro, and moved to Edgecombe County in 1894. His brother-in-law Henry Cheatham had already represented the Second District, also referred to as "The Black Second" because of its high population of African Americans. George White was elected in 1896 and 1898 and was the last African American to serve in

Congress until just before World War II. In his last term, he was the only African American in Congress and still was unsuccessful in passing an anti-lynching bill. In 1901, he delivered his last speech, announcing that the Black man would rise phoenix-like in American politics. A strong white supremacist movement to disenfranchise Blacks in North Carolina caused White to lose the 1900 election. He left North Carolina in 1901, moved to Washington D.C., and then established a community in New Jersey called Whitesboro. His home on Granville Street in Tarboro is still standing.

One of Carr's first acts as governor was to select someone to represent the state at the Columbian Exhibition World's Fair in Chicago. Carr chose his neighbor Sally Southall Cotten, wife of Robert Cotten—a former Tarboro merchant who had purchased a plantation just across the county line. Sally created an exhibit featuring North Carolina writers and history. A major part of the exhibit was the Virginia Dare Desk, which featured holly wood panels carved by Katherine "Kate" Drane Cheshire. The panels depicted the legend of Virginia Dare as a white doe, Sir Walter Raleigh's coat-of-arms, and the scuppernong vine native to North Carolina.

Kate Cheshire, the daughter of the rector, was a skilled artist. Except for the years at St. Mary's College in Raleigh, she spent her entire life in Tarboro. She

The North Carolina exhibit at the Columbian Exposition in Chicago of 1893–1894 featured a hand-carved desk by Katherine Cheshire. Panels showed the royal crests and the Roanoke Island settlement—giving it the name "The Virginia Dare Desk," honoring the first English child born in the new world. Kate Cheshire was a talented artist of painted tiles, carved fireplace mantels, and church altars, and other decorative items. (Courtesy of North Carolina Office of Archives and History.)

painted pottery and tiles and created ink drawings in her small studio on Church Street, but was most expert at wood carving. She carved the altar at Grace Episcopal Church in Lawrence and the font cover and chalice box used at Calvary. She also made mantels, often featuring animal designs, for several homes in Tarboro. She was active in her church, helped to establish Grace Church and taught school there for many years, and served as secretary and president of the Woman's Auxiliary of the Diocese. Kate Cheshire died in 1935.

GROWING INDUSTRY AND AGRICULTURE

The industrial movement to rebuild the South after Reconstruction had a positive effect in Edgecombe County. An 1891 promotional tract entitled *Edgecombe County North Carolina: Her People and Resources. The Foremost Agricultural Section of the State* highlighted the area:

> There are three printing establishments, banking, insurance, building and loan, express and telegraph facilities, saw, planing and grist-mills, agricultural implements, iron and machine works, blacksmithing, brick-yards, buggy carriage, and harness factories.

Printing establishments included several newspapers. In 1884, there were four weeklies in the county: the *Tarboro Southerner*; the *Guide*, a Democratic paper; the *Rocky Mount Mail*, another Democratic paper; and the *NC Sentinel*, a Republican paper edited by African American John C. Dancy. Two other papers circulated during the decade, the *Carolina Banner*, and the *Farmer's Advocate*. Rocky Mount

Runnymede Mills was one of several textile mills in Tarboro at the turn of the twentieth century. A mill village provided homes for the workers. (Courtesy of North Carolina Office of Archives and History.)

The county seat of Tarboro was very busy, as indicated in this 1907 street scene. People came to town for court or for business, such as selling cotton or tobacco. The building on the left with the balcony is the O.C. Farrar Hotel on the corner of St. George (Main Street) and St. James Streets. (Courtesy of Blount-Bridgers House Archives.)

witnessed a second paper, the *Phoenix*. The *Southerner*, which was established by George Howard and continued by his son, survived all the competition and became a daily in the twentieth century, but not without several changes in editors. Frank Powell assumed the reins of the paper in 1881, after Dossey Battle owned it for six years.

Numerous businesses opened during the 1880s and 1890s. The Royster Guano Plant, established in 1885 by F.S. Royster, became one of the largest fertilizer companies in the south. Eventually Royster moved his headquarters to Norfolk, but the company returned to Tarboro in the 1980s. O.C. Farrar opened Hotel Farrar on the corner of Main and St. James Streets in 1887. Later he promoted it as "the Worst Hotel in the State." The three-story structure featured stores on the main floor with hotel rooms upstairs. Edgecombe Homestead & Loan was founded by S.S. Nash in 1889. Greek immigrant Nick Constantine opened a candy factory in 1891. The Tarboro Chewing Gum Company began in 1894.

The biggest change to the area was the increase in textile mills. Tarboro Cotton Mills opened in 1888. The corporation was funded by various investors, the largest of which was O.C. Farrar with $10, 000, followed by R.H. Austin, Dr. N.J. Pittman, and Dennis Simmons with $5,000 each. Other investors contributed between $100 and $2,500. An electric plant was built near the cotton mill to supply the power. When it was in full operation, the mill employed over 125 people. In 1889, John Shackelford built Riverview Knitting Mills, which employed 80 people. Just ten years later, Runnymede Mills opened.

Completed in the 1880s, the Redmond-Shackleford House is considered one of the best examples of Second Empire architecture in North Carolina. Located on the corner of Pitt and Main Streets, the three-story brick house was stuccoed to look like stone. (Courtesy of Historic Preservation of Edgecombe County, Blount-Bridgers House Archives.)

The 1890s also saw the development of tobacco as an economic resource. The first warehouse opened in Tarboro in 1891; others soon appeared in Battleboro and Rocky Mount. In the first year, over 60,000 pounds were sold—causing some to speculate that tobacco would replace cotton as the main crop. Eventually it did, but it was neighboring Pitt and Wilson Counties that became the largest tobacco markets in the world in the twentieth century.

Residents began building homes along Main Street north of the common all the way to the train depot. In 1890, the new Tarboro Town Hall was built by George Matthewson, an African-American carpenter. The two-story structure featured a bell tower and had town offices, the jail, and the fire department on the first floor, with an opera house on the second floor. The town began to boast suburbs of Hilmaville, West Tarboro, Dancy Field, and the Depot. Within the decade, two mill villages cropped up. The Old Town and churchyard cemeteries were filling, so a new cemetery called Oakland was established on Howard Avenue.

By 1898, Henry Clark Bridgers built the East Carolina Railway running south to Hookerton in Greene County. This line led to the development of such towns as Pinetops and Macclesfield, and to the demise of Old Sparta—as railways became preferred over shipping. The Atlantic Coast Railroad also selected Rocky Mount as the site for its repair shops in 1899, providing a tremendous boost to that area. According to the promotional tract, crops grown in Edgecombe included:

cotton, corn, wheat, oats, rice, barley, sorghum or amber sugar-cane, tobacco, peanuts, broomcorn, field peas, clover, hay, beans, ramie, flax, buck wheat, sweet potatoes, Irish potatoes, basket- willow, all varieties of beats including the sugar-beat, melons, castor-bean, sun-flower, try, chufas and some others of less value. The staple crop of the present cultivation is cotton. In this crop the per acre yield of Edgecombe leads except some counties in Miss. and Louisiana. The annual product is from 25,000 to 30,000 bales.

The area also had a strong crop of peanuts. A four-story factory was constructed to handle and clean the legumes. Other produce included pears, apples, peaches, plums, cherries, strawberries, raspberries, currants, gooseberries, and cranberry vines. Timber included pine, beechwood, persimmon, cypress, and oak. In addition to growing crops, several dairy farms excelled in the production of butter and milk:

> More than 35,000 pounds of butter will be made in this county and sold this year. . . . J.C. Powell from Coolmore will sell more than 3,000 lbs for 40¢ and Mrs. John L. Bridgers . . . 2,000 lbs from 8 cows. Charles King and Panola Farm furnish the town with milk twice a day for 5¢ a qt.

A steam locomotive leaves the Rocky Mount depot in this image. Atlantic Coast Line relocated its repair shops and headquarters to Rocky Mount in 1899, greatly expanding the town's population. (Courtesy of North Carolina Office of Archives and History.)

Overall, the agricultural worth of Edgecombe County was estimated at $2.5 million.

FIRES AND INSPIRATION

Several fires in Edgecombe County during the 1890s and early 1900s caused considerable damage. The Female Academy on the town common burned on January 1, 1891. By the time the fire was discovered at 1:30 a.m., only some furniture could be saved before the building was destroyed. Fortunately, students were not in session, so there were no injuries. The Male Academy, housed in the original academy building constructed in 1813, had burned in November 1885.

A more serious fire burned much of Princeville in October 1893. Beginning in a stable, the fire consumed four stores, a restaurant, a butcher shop, a barber shop, and the stable. At the time, Princeville did not have a fire department and the Tarboro Fire Company saved the nearby homes.

Another fire destroyed several businesses on the west 400 block of Main Street. This fire completely engulfed the Bryan House, formerly Mrs. Gregory's Hotel. Nearby businesses also suffered serious damage. A newspaper published a few days after the fire featured a letter from a merchant thanking the citizens for

The MacNair Drug Store located on the 400 block of Main Street was destroyed by fire in 1897, but reopened with a better establishment featuring a soda fountain. (Courtesy of North Carolina Office of Archives and History.)

saving the stock in his store by dragging much of it into the street. The store was a total loss, but at least he was able to salvage some of his dry goods. As the fire threatened much of the business district, a telegram was sent to Rocky Mount asking for help. Forty-two minutes later, a special train arrived to help battle the blaze, which by that time was under control.

On a Friday afternoon in May 1900, just as the Tar River Mills was closing, a cry of fire alerted everyone. The sawmill and lumber yard located across the river from Tarboro were covered in dense smoke with flames leaping over 100 feet into the air. Workers struggled to save some of the stacked lumber and keep it from being more fuel for the blaze. Both the Tarboro and Princeville fire departments responded. Despite the hard work that saved several structures, damages to mill machinery totaled over $12,500.

The last major fire occurred in the early morning of December 19, 1901. Riverview Knitting Mills—which had been operating for 12 years—was completely burned to the ground, leaving over a hundred people out of work. The loss of equipment and materials was estimated at $50,000.

Although both the Male and Female Academies had burned, education in the county did not cease. Frank Wilkinson, the teacher and principal of the Male Academy since 1858, opened a new school in his home and continued to instruct students there after the academy burned. A graduate of the University of North Carolina, Wilkinson was an Edgecombe native that demanded much from his students. He taught them the classics; his graduates were fluent in Greek and Latin and were admitted to the University of North Carolina without taking entrance exams. Many of his students were successful leaders of the state, becoming lawyers, judges, politicians, historians, and even an Episcopal bishop. Wilkinson became the first superintendent of public schools in the county, and it was his job to visit regularly the numerous public schools that had been created throughout the county. In the spring of 1888, he visited the "Free School for Colored People," which averaged over 200 students a day. Old Man Frank, as he was known, spent over 60 years of his life as an educator in Edgecombe County, retiring shortly before his death in 1919.

County records for 1896 identify 34 white public schools and 37 for black students. In addition to the Tarboro Academies, there were private schools in Whitakers, Rocky Mount, Battleboro, and Rocky Mount. Perhaps the most successful was located in the Bricks community north of Whitakers. The Joseph K. Bricks Junior College for African-Americans opened in 1895. Bricks educated a large number of students from across the country using the Tuskeegee model. He taught academics, while requiring students to work on campus in the kitchen, the dining room, or the large garden. Supported by the American Missionary Association, Bricks was forced to close during the Depression. For a short time in World War II, its buildings were used for a public school.

Along with schools, churches also popped up across the county. The only Catholic church, St. Catherine's, began in 1898. Several other denominations also built houses of worship: Temperance Hall Methodist in 1884, St. Mary's

Soldiers from Edgecombe County have served in all American wars. This monument on the town common commemorates the service of those in the Spanish-American War from 1898 to 1900. John W. Cotten was captain of Company I of the 2nd North Carolina Volunteers. Other local soldiers included Privates John Godley and Samuel Johnson, who died in the war, and Sergeants William Baker, Joseph Warrant, Charles Jenkins, William Sugg, Thomas Gatling, and Walter Simmons.

Episcopal Mission in Speed in 1883, Hart's Chapel in 1891, Washington Branch Missionary Baptist in 1900, Macclesfield Christian Church in 1905, Eastern Star Baptist in 1907, Union Baptist in 1908, Pines Chapel in 1909, and Pentecostal Holiness Church in 1911.

Locally, citizens were in a positive era of growth and development with schools, churches, and the influx of immigrants establishing new businesses, but national events cast a cloud: the threat of another war loomed. Newspapers focused attention on the political unrest in Cuba and the country's relationship with Spain. The United States sent the battleship *Maine* to Cuba, resulting in the United States engaging in a war with Spain in 1898. As in previous national wars, Edgecombe sent troops to the Spanish-American War. The 2nd North Carolina Regiment was composed of 12 companies. Company I, headed by Tarboro police chief Major John Whitaker Cotten, mustered in on May 15. They were sent to St. Augustine, Florida to prepare to go to Cuba. Cotten was soon discharged and returned home, while Captain Carl W. Jeffries of the Edgecombe Guards assumed command. Willliam Baker of Tarboro was the first sergeant. Other area soldiers included Warren, Jenkins, Sugg, Gatling, Simmons, Laurence, Peters, and Hussey. Although they never saw action in Cuba, several men—including John Godly and

Samuel Johnson, both of Tarboro—died while in camp from diseases such as typhoid and measles.

THE NEW CENTURY

At the end of the nineteenth century, Tarboro had almost 2,500 citizens, approximately one-tenth of the county's population of over 26,500. Rocky Mount had grown from 800 to almost 3,000 aided by the Atlantic Coastline Railroad (ACL). The Rocky Mount Mill village alone had a population of over 600. In the first 20 years of the twentieth century, Edgecombe County witnessed a tremendous growth in population and industry, as railroads changed its economic structure. Citizens learned new skills to work in the numerous factories. Schools quadrupled to serve the young population. New towns sprang up along the rail lines, signaling the beginning of the decline of some older river communities.

Pinetops and Macclesfield were both products of the East Carolina Railway, which ran from Tarboro south into Greene County. Henry C. Bridgers named the area Macclesfield after what he believed was the Bridgers family ancestral home in England. The town was incorporated in 1901 and had a post office by the next year. Pinetops came along just two years later and soon surpassed Macclesfield in size and population. In 1904, Pinetops got its first bank and by 1915, had two churches (Methodist and Presbyterian), one school, one jeweler, eight stores, a drugstore, two hotels, and one doctor. Pinetops Sash and Blind Company, the

St. Lewis School in western Edgecombe County was one of the 70 community schools in the county in the 1920s. (Courtesy of North Carolina Office of Archives and History.)

Pinetops Oil and Guano Company, and W.L. Dunn employed most of the population of about 300.

The community of Knights Station in the eastern edge of the county was renamed Speed in 1901 to honor Dr. E.T. Speed. In 1915, Speed was the smallest Edgecombe community with about 70 residents. After Tarboro, Whitakers was the largest town with over 1,000 people. Many of the residents worked for the Hearn Brothers Coffin Company or Southern Hardware Manufacturing Company. Leggett was another community that grew north of the county seat. It was named for Henry Leggett, who served in both the Civil and Spanish American Wars.

Businesses continued to increase along with the population. The Pittman Memorial Hospital opened in 1901 to serve Edgecombe residents. ACL opened the second hospital in the area the following year. Fountain Cotton Mills opened in 1902, providing jobs for those who had worked at Riverview Mills. There were over a dozen cotton gins and four cotton oil companies in the county by 1905, indicating tobacco had not replaced cotton as the major crop. There were 19 saloons until 1913, when North Carolina enacted Prohibition. The first soft drink–bottling plant in the area was opened by the Brown family in 1912 and sold Coca-Cola. Marrow-Pitt Hardware was established in 1913 on Main Street. The Red Gum Veneer Company began in 1916. In 1918, Tarboro opened the first municipally-owned milk plant in the country, providing pasteurized milk to its

The wife of a British officer, Edgecombe native Madelon Battle Hancock served at Antwerpt in 1914 and earned the name "Glory" for her dedication to the soldiers. She was mentioned in a 1915 article in the Saturday Evening Post by Mary Roberts Rinehart, who called her "Morning Glory, a Southern girl." (Courtesy of the Edward B. Lewis family.)

A popular sporting event here in the early twentieth century was horseracing. Others included minor league baseball games. (Courtesy of North Carolina Office of Archives and History.)

residents. The following year, North Carolina's first regional health department originated in Edgecombe County.

Two sports, new to the area, provided entertainment. Baseball became the national pastime, and was enjoyed in Edgecombe as well. Local teams played on the town common, and by 1909, Rocky Mount had organized a minor league team, the Rocky Mount Railroaders. All-American Jim Thorpe played one season on this team. That same year, the local Tarboro team played against the Cherokee Indians in a double-header. The second game of the double-header was the first in this region to be played "under the lights," as electric lights were put up by the field. Golf also became a popular form of recreation. In the 1890s, John Luther Bridgers Jr. laid out a nine-hole course near his home, Hilma. By 1902, the West Tarboro Golf Club formed. Its bylaws accepted both men and ladies.

WORLD WAR I

Over 1,000 men from Edgecombe County served in World War I. Nine died in action and five were among 200 North Carolinians to receive the distinguished service cross for bravery. Local soldiers included Sergeant Sam R. Brown of Company F, 322nd infantry; Sergeant Thomas Carlisle of Company D, 119th infantry; 1st Lieutenant Thomas H. Royster in the medical corp of the 30th infantry; Corporal Garland Spain of Company E 322nd infantry; and Corporal Charles F. Stephenson of Company D of the 105th engineers. Other decorated World War I servicemen included Spencer Hart and Commander Adolphus

Staton. The last received a Congressional Medal of Honor for action in a marine assault at Vera Cruz in 1914. Staton had attended both the Virginia Military Academy and the University of North Carolina and graduated from the U.S. Naval Academy. In World War I, he was the executive officer of the U.S.S. *Mount Vernon*. When that ship was torpedoed, Staton was awarded the Navy Cross. In 1920, he was appointed commander of the battleship U.S.S *Tennessee*. In the 1920s, Staton served in the Pacific fleet. He was an instructor at the Command and General Staff School in Fort Leavenworth, Kansas in 1935. Although he retired in 1937, he was called back to active duty in World War II. He retired a second time at the end of World War II with the rank of rear admiral. Staton died in 1964 and was buried with military honors in Arlington National Cemetery.

Women joined the war effort as nurses, often working for the Red Cross rather than the United States military. A Red Cross nursing group in Rocky Mount made bandages. One member stood above the rest: Madelon Battle Hancock of Edgecombe County became the most decorated woman in the war for her outstanding service to soldiers under fire. Madelon married Mortimer Pawson Hancock of Great Britain, who was a major general in the British Army at the onset of the war. An article in the April 8, 1920 *Tarboro Daily Southerner* told her story:

Although the United States did not enter World War I until 1917, Americans were serving in various capacities. Madelon "Glory" Battle Hancock from Edgecombe County became a Red Cross nurse and served throughout the war in field hospitals at the fronts in Belgium and France. (Courtesy of the Edward B. Lewis family.)

Mrs. Hancock is known in the whole British army as "Glory Hancock," a name which she won by her untiring and earnest work in the ranks of the Red Cross during the recent great war against Germany. She went to Antwerpt, in Belgium, August 13, 1914, only a few days after the war began with the first British field hospital, not only to enter that part of the war stricken country but in fact the first British field hospital to take service in the front lines, in Belgium. She remained there until October 12 of the same year, when during the retreat by the Allies she brought in under fire many wounded Belgians and British, the latter of the Royal Naval Division.

She was then attached to the hospital established at Fermes, in Belgium, and nursed there through the first battle of the Yser, when the hospital was shelled by the Germans and had to be evacuated, the patients being moved to Hoogstadt, where Mrs. Hancock was stationed during the first and second battles of Ypres and the second battle of the Marne.

Until the last battle of the war, Mrs. Hancock was at the above named and other dressing stations close behind the Allied lines of battle until the last moment of the war; never being beyond the sound of the guns and frequently within the zone of fire. She was gassed, was repeatedly in the midst of shrapnel fire but always escaped without serious injury.

For her services to the wounded and her conspicuous bravery under fire upon various occasions Mrs. Hancock received twelve decorations, five from Great Britain, five from Belgium and two from France. Those from Great Britain are: The Mons Star, Royal Red Cross, Allied Service Medal, British Victory Medal and King George V Medal, the latter personally given by His Majesty. Those from Belgium are the Chevalier de Pordre de la Cpuronne, (crown) personally given by King Albert and carrying with it the title of countess; Criux de Guerre, Order of the Yser. Order of Queen Elizabeth, Civic Cross. From France: Croix de Guerre, Medal a Reconnoissance pour les Estrangers.

The July 7, 1919 *Norfolk Virginia-Pilot* described a large enthusiastic July Fourth parade that honored the veterans of World War I. A victory arch over Main Street provided the entrance for the floats and cars in the parade. Three companies of soldiers, one of sailors, and one of African-American troops all marched and were showered with flowers by the residents who lined the streets. Veterans from previous wars wore their uniforms as well. After the parade, people enjoyed a barbeque dinner and watched horse races at the fairgrounds. A late afternoon baseball game between Enfield and Tarboro ended in a victory for the home team. At 9 o'clock, a street dance began with the Black citizens segregated at one end of the street and the whites on the other end. The report concluded, "never has a better-behaved crowed assembled together . . . for the wonderfully successful occasion."

5. GROWING PAINS 1920–1960

The federal census in 1920 revealed that Edgecombe County had a total population of 37,995—an increase of over 5,000 since the previous census and almost 10,000 since the turn of the century. In 1900, Tarboro had 2,500 citizens. By 1920, its population had almost doubled to 4,568 people. Immigrants settling in Tarboro accounted for part of the increase. At least 12 different native languages were used by Tarboro residents, most of whom had migrated to the United States within the past 20 years. In addition to the Swiss and Jewish immigrants of the 1870s and 1880s, new foreign residents included a Chinese laundry owner, two Greek restaurant owners, an Italian weaver, a Hawaiian cook, a housekeeper from Scotland, a teacher from the West Indies, a store manager from Sweden, an Arabic family from Syria, a musician from Germany, and several salesmen and merchants from Russia and Poland.

Even though Rocky Mount had three times the population of Tarboro, reaching almost 13,000, the city did not have as many foreign residents. It did, however, have five Greek families and several Jewish families from Poland, Austria, and Lithuania. There were also immigrants from Ireland, England, and France—most of whom worked for the railroad, the major employer in Rocky Mount.

Community interest was focused on education throughout the 1920s. Tarboro opened a new high school in 1922, and the first Parent Teacher Association was also organized in that year. The largest expenditure of the county budget—just over half a million dollars—went to the public school system. The public schools had almost 5,000 students with over half of them, 2,824, African Americans. The students attended one of 20 white schools or 22 schools for African Americans. Between 1910 and 1932, philanthropist Julius Rosenwald—president of Sears, Roebuck and Company—established a fund to provide plans and matching funds to southern African-American communities who wanted a school. It is estimated that 800 such schools were built in North Carolina. Fifteen of those Rosenwald-funded schools were constructed in Edgecombe County. Attendance ranged from a high of 270 students in Pinetops to a low of 30 students in Sparta. Eight other schools in the district were closed or combined as part of a consolidation effort. South Edgecombe was consolidated in 1926 with a new building. The next year, West Edgecombe was the largest consolidated school in the state.

Higher education was also encouraged and recognized in the area. In 1927, over 40 students from the county were attending colleges—33 in state at the University of North Carolina, St. Mary's, Davidson, North Carolina College for Women, and North Carolina State University. Others could be found at Yale, the U.S. Naval Academy, Virginia Military Institute, Washington & Lee University, University of Maryland, and University of Richmond.

In 1920, the 19th Amendment gave women the right to vote. North Carolina had the opportunity to be the 36th state to ratify the amendment, but voted against it. Regardless, women became involved in local politics. In 1924, Miss Mary Ballard Bunn of Tarboro became the first woman elected register of deeds in North Carolina. That year also saw the second-worst flood in the recorded history of the county, a major Klan rally on the Tarboro common, and the opening of an airport. Lieutenant William "Phil" Fillmore, a World War I ace, operated the J.M. Baker Flying Field to provide residents with modern transportation to Washington, D.C. and other destinations.

George Holderness moved to Tarboro in 1888 as a salesman. He and W.H. Powell organized the Tarboro Telephone Company in 1895. Within two years, it grew from 75 lines to over 150, and became Carolina Telephone and Telegraph—with exchanges throughout eastern North Carolina. The company

Edgecombe County Superintendent Mr. Sentell (standing in the back) visits one of the 37 African-American schools in the county in 1925. At least 14 of the schools were Rosenwald schools. (Courtesy of North Carolina Office of Archives and History.)

In the 1930s, the county acquired the Blount-Bridgers House as a community center and, with a WPA grant, constructed the first municipal swimming pool behind the house. Tarboro residents enjoyed the pool until it closed in the 1980s. (Courtesy of Edgecombe County Memorial Library.)

covered Washington, Kinston, Fayetteville, and many other communities. In 1926, the company merged with the Home T&T in Henderson; Tarboro became the home office. Soon the company expanded to 35 counties in North Carolina.

During the "Great Tar River Flood of 1924," the river crested at 32.3 feet—just a foot under the record set in 1919 when Princeville had been virtually destroyed. Particularly cautious after the previous flood, people moved from low-lying areas in 1924. Several bridges—including the railroad bridge—were washed out, halting transportation. In more disastrous weather news, a severe thunderstorm in August caused a lightning strike and resulting fire that destroyed St. Paul's Baptist Church.

In December, hundreds of people, both Black and white, lined the streets to witness a Ku Klux Klan parade. The December 10, 1924 *Daily Southerner* reported the group marched down Main Street from the Tar River bridge and collected at the town common around an electric cross. The speaker from Kinston and most other members removed their hoods. Membership cards distributed during the rally littered the common the next morning, although the speaker had indicated that all were welcome to join the Klan, which was "100% American and not anti-Jew, anti-Catholic, nor anti-Negro." The paper reported that "many of the colored people of the town paid strict attention to the address."

A blizzard and a tornado left their mark on Edgecombe County in 1927. Over a decade had passed since the county had experienced a major winter storm. Then on March 2, Edgecombe residents went to bed with a forecast of rain and awoke to over a foot of snow, which continued to fall throughout the day. Wind blew drifts to 4-5 feet and the *Southerner* reported, "streets are almost impassable and automobiles that were left on the street last night were hard to move." Trains were canceled all the way to Norfolk because the tracks were covered in snow drifts of up to 7 feet. Later that year, a tornado ravaged the area, blowing away part of Hart Cotton Mill and destroying several homes in Tarboro. Fortunately, no fatalities were reported.

Bad weather could not deter the faith of Edgecombe residents. The new First Baptist Church of Tarboro on Main Street was dedicated in 1928. Although it was one of the largest churches in the county, it could not hold the crowd for a special service in the spring of 1928. Instead, evangelist Billy Sunday, visiting from Greenville, addressed a standing-room-only crowd at the county courthouse. The May 25, 1928 *Daily Southerner* reported that Sunday "held his audience spellbound" with a "a most eloquent and convincing" message. Local ministers Yearby from the Baptist church and Reverend Bertram Brown from Calvary Episcopal Church were also part of the special service. Worshippers came from all around the county to hear the well-known evangelist.

THE DEPRESSION

The 1930s are traditionally remembered as the Great Depression. Unemployment was high, companies went out of business, and people reverted to homemade items. Fortunately, Edgecombe County benefited from several government programs. A new concrete bridge was built across the Tar River connecting Tarboro and Princeville. The town of Tarboro used WPA funds to purchase the Blount House and turned it into a community center with a swimming pool behind the house. The pool provided training for a local swim team, which won 21 medals in the 1937 Southeast Regional Competition in Atlanta. The Municipal Ball Park was built on Panola Street across from the public school, now C.B. Martin Middle School. The county also gained some new buildings, a water treatment facility on Albemarle Avenue, an agricultural extension office, and a courthouse annex. Sidewalks and gutters were installed in Whitakers, Rocky Mount, Pinetops, and Tarboro neighborhoods. The new County Poor House was relocated to north Main Street with four wings to house residents and an upstairs apartment for director Mattie Shackelford.

Perhaps one of the most beneficial changes for county residents was the availability of electricity. The Edgecombe-Martin Electric Co-op was formed in 1937 to provide electricity throughout the county. For the first time, county residents had not only electric lights, but some had household appliances such as radios, electric washing machines, and refrigerators. One farm woman praised the electric freezer, which made saving food less time-consuming than when she had to cook and can the fruits and vegetables in Mason jars. Another benefit for farm families was the development of a farmer's market. Families could sell or purchase homegrown vegetables, fresh game, chickens, eggs, wood, and homemade foods like butter and jelly. The money earned could then be used to purchase store-bought materials not available on the farm.

Government programs also provided employment for area citizens. Some surveyed old cemeteries. Others worked in the new school lunchrooms preparing food grown in school gardens during the summer. Some kept records in the courthouse. Some women made clothes for the needy in sewing groups. Others volunteered in literacy programs or operated a book mobile.

The WPA also developed state travel books describing all the communities near state and federal highways. The *WPA Guide to North Carolina*, published in 1939, described Princeville and Tarboro. Princeville was recognized for having the only all-African-American administration, including a volunteer fire company, in the state. Tarboro was described as a:

> tobacco-selling and cotton-manufacturing center. The principle crops are cotton, tobacco, and peanuts; Tarboro manufactures cotton cloth, cottonseed products, veneers, corn meal, and feed. The municipality operates a creamery and maintains a high standard for its milk supply.

Dozens of cars surround the railroad depot and warehouse, located at the corner of Howard Avenue and north Main Street, in the late 1920s. The Edgecombe County Historical Society fought to save part of this complex in 1997. (Courtesy of Edgecombe County Memorial Library.)

Hanging and curing tobacco was a labor-intensive process involving most farmers in Edgecombe County in the first half of the twentieth century. (Courtesy of North Carolina Office of Archives and History.)

The guide also described the oldest standing structure in the county, known as the Bark House. Located on Wilson Street, the frame structure reportedly dated to the 1720s.

Despite the Depression, there was sufficient capital and support for several new enterprises. Bell's Cleaning Plant opened just before the stock market crash. Ford cars could be purchased at the newly-opened Tarboro Motor Company. This provided shoppers a choice, as the Enterprise Carriage Company opened by Thad Hussey in 1866, now sold Chevrolets, Oldsmobiles, and Buicks. The Tarboro Knitting Mills were bought out by the Mayo family, who continued to operate the mill into the next century. Adler's Cash Store opened in 1931, selling a complete line of clothes for men, women, and children. H&P Mercantile Store opened in 1933 as the most complete and fanciest grocery store in the area. The Tarboro Merchants Association was created to promote and support downtown businesses. Pinetops saw the Cotton Belt Manufacturing Company open in 1936. At the end of the decade, the Edgecombe Casket Company opened in an old tobacco warehouse in Pinetops.

Local events that captured attention included an unusual wedding setting. On August 8, 1931, Miss Tamsie Harrell of Tarboro and Otey Pollard of Rocky Mount were married in the front window of Simmons Furniture Store in Tarboro at 9:30 in the evening. Not only was the town invited, but announcements went out

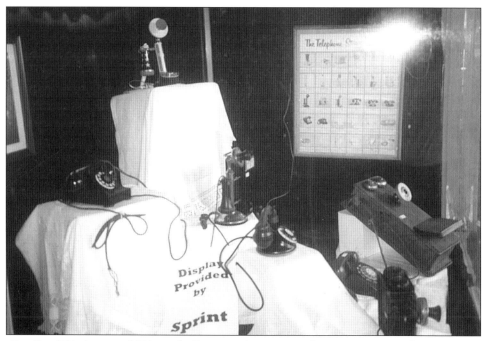

Carolina Telephone and Telegraph Company began in Tarboro in 1896. By the 1970s, the company was part of United Telecom and by the 1990s, it was part of Sprint. This display of old phones was put in an empty storefront on Main Street to remind the community of its connection to telephone history.

through the eastern part of the state to witness this unique wedding. In July 1935, alcohol became legally available for the first time in over 20 years. (North Carolina had passed prohibition in 1912, years before the country did.) Sheriff Tom Bardin and a federal revenue tax collector were on hand to make sure the regulations were followed.

The *Southerner* celebrated its 110th anniversary in 1934; a special edition of the paper gave a detailed description of the area's growth. Tarboro had a Pepsi-Cola Bottling Works managed by B.F. Taylor that sold Pepsi, Seven-Up, and Orange Julep. The Colonial Theatre had opened in 1919 and created competition with the Opera House for providing feature films. Residents had several drug stores to choose from. Zoeller's (formerly Staton & Zoeller) had been operating for over 50 years. The owner, Dr. E.V. Zoeller, was also president of the North Carolina Board of Pharmacy, a position he held for 35 years. Cook's Drug Store was located in the Masonic Building on the corner of Main and Pitt Streets. The Edgecombe Drug Company sold drugs and household items and featured Columbia Records for listening pleasure.

The largest employers in the county were still the textile mills, specifically Fountain Cotton Mills and Hart Cotton Mills, which was originally the Tarboro Cotton Mills. Another large employer was Carolina Telephone and Telegraph, which operated 77 exchanges throughout the eastern half of the state. The Columbian Peanut Company operated 27 plants in the South, with the first being the Tarboro plant that opened in 1893.

The *Southerner* also had a new editor to replace Paul Jones, who had served since 1923. Before Jones, the paper had been edited by Frank Powell who changed the weekly to a daily paper in 1889. Jones had to retire due to illness, and was replaced by Bertram H. Brown. Brown left in 1937 and Aubrey Shackell succeeded him.

August 19, 1930 was the date of the last reported lynching in the area. A man accused of raping two children was taken from the Edgecombe County jail to the farm on the Edgecombe-Wilson County line where the alleged rapes occurred. His "bullet-riddled" body was discovered the next morning. Despite investigation by the local and state police, no arrests were made.

In the1930s, Edgecombe County lost two of its spiritual leaders. Bishop Joseph Blount Cheshire died in December 1932 at the age of 82. Bishop Cheshire was the son of J.B. Cheshire, rector of Calvary Episcopal Church for over 50 years. The bishop was active in his hometown as well as the state. He helped establish St. Peter's Hospital in Charlotte and the Good Samaritan Hospital, the first hospital for Blacks in North Carolina. While bishop, he helped the church acquire St. Mary's, a private girls' school that had opened in Raleigh in 1842. Cheshire encouraged the Episcopal Church to take over the school and it became the largest Episcopal school for girls in the United States. He wrote several volumes of church and local history; the last, *Nonulla*, was published just two years before his death. Cheshire was also active in the North Carolina Literary and Historical Association. He died in Charlotte and his remains were brought home to Tarboro and buried in the family plot in Calvary Churchyard. Reverend Bertram E. Brown, rector of Calvary Church, died in 1937. Reverend Brown was responsible for establishing several mission churches in the county.

For the third time in 21 years, the Tar River overflowed its banks in August 1940, cresting at 31 feet and causing the evacuation of Princeville and other low-lying communities. Over 100 families in Princeville took themselves and their belongings to higher ground. Deep Creek also flooded the community of Speed, forcing 25 families to temporarily relocate. Some roads and bridges were closed and traffic redirected. Bell's Bridge on the main highway was under several feet of water, causing those in Leggett and east to go through Rocky Mount to get to Tarboro. There was no damage in Rocky Mount, and the flood waters receded within a few days.

The 1940s witnessed several changes in medical care. In 1940, the new Edgecombe General Hospital was built on St. Andrew Street next to St. James Methodist Church on the site of the old Pittman Hospital, which had been torn down. The Tarboro Clinic, formed in 1928, occupied the first floor. A home for nurses was built on St. Patrick Street behind the new hospital.

In 1936, Dr. Milton Quigless moved to Tarboro and set up practice. He was the second African-American doctor in the area, following Dr. Alexander McMillan. On December 1, 1946, Dr. Quigless opened the first hospital in the county to serve African Americans. The Quigless Clinic and Hospital, located on the corner of Main and Water Streets, was furnished with surplus military equipment. The two-story brick structure included the doctor's office, an X-ray department, waiting rooms, and treatment rooms. The second floor had a large ward for women and a smaller ward for men along with a nursery for children. The hospital served both Black and white citizens until it closed in 1975. Dr. Quigless remained in practice until 1997.

After World War II, Dr. Quigless became active in community affairs. In the spring of 1946, he organized the Negro Civic League and became its first president. The March 30, 1946 *Daily Southerner* reported that this organization aimed to "develop cooperation among the colored citizens of Tarboro" and promote "better inter-racial understanding." It also organized programs to provide productive outlets for young people and curb juvenile delinquency.

Edgecombe County's population grew since the beginning of the century, and by 1940 numbered 49,162. Rocky Mount was the largest town in the twin counties with over 25,000 citizens, making it one of the ten largest cities in the state. Tarboro gained almost 1,000 residents since the 1930 census and registered 7,148 inhabitants.

Dr. Milton Quigless opened the Quigless Hospital in Tarboro in the late 1940s because segregation would not allow his patients in the county hospital. Much of his equipment had been World War II surplus material. Although the hospital closed in 1975, Dr. Quigless continued to see patients in his office until 1997. The North Carolina Museum of History used this room from his hospital for a health and healing display that opened in 1998. (Courtesy of North Carolina Museum of History.)

WORLD WAR II

World War II occupied the minds of most citizens. Over ten percent of the county population—almost 5,000 men—served in the army, navy, or marines. Women served in the Women's Army Corps (WACs) or the Red Cross. Even those at home were engaged in the war effort. Local farmers grew tobacco that was made into Lucky Strike cigarettes by the R.J. Reynolds Tobacco Company and sent to soldiers overseas. Children collected stamps to buy war bonds and scrap metal.

The *Home Front News* was published by the Tarboro Rotary Club from 1942 to 1945. It kept all the service people informed as to what was happening in Edgecombe County. The staff of W.S. Babcock, H. Dail Holderness, and Jim Simmons Jr. collected information about who enlisted and where they were stationed. Often, the paper could only identify whereabouts as "somewhere in the Pacific" or "somewhere in France," so as not to reveal information to the enemy. The writers also reported local weddings, births, and community news. By the end of 1942, circulation grew from 700 to over 1,000. By the end of the war, over 2,000 people were receiving copies of the 18–20 page monthly newspaper. Early papers were illustrated by Alice Evans and later issues featured photos by M.S. Brown, owner of the local Coca-Cola Company. Some soldiers indicated that next to family letters, the *Home Front News* was what they looked most forward to receiving.

News from home included a report of a heat wave in August 1942, which set a record high temperature of 107 degrees. In November 1942, Movietone News filmed Tarboro High School faculty and staff harvesting crops. The Tarboro Kiwanis club sold $60,000 worth of bonds and stamps to aid the war effort. Many servicemen and women passed through Rocky Mount on the trains. A service men's organization (similar to the U.S.O.) was established and in just four months provided food to over 10,000 soldiers. In the summer of 1943, the hardware and ladies departments of W.S. Clark & Sons were destroyed by fire.

Over 400 women from the county served in active military duty or with the Red Cross. Joyce Denson of Rocky Mount joined her two brothers in the navy by enlisting in the U.S. Navy Women's Reserve, or WAVES (Women Accepted for Volunteer Emergency Service). Mrs. Glanor Best and Mrs. Marion Wall of Tarboro were the first to join the WACs in 1942. Soon the *Home Front News* listed new WACs in each issue. Mary Ferebee Howard went to Washington, D.C. and joined the Red Cross. She was stationed in the Pacific at New Caledonia and Guadalcanal, operating the service club. After the war, she earned her B.S. and M.A. from East Carolina University and taught school in Tarboro and Rocky Mount. Mary's two brothers, Lieutenant Commander Stamps Howard and Lieutenant Nelson Howard, also served in the navy.

Martha Westray Battle Boyce came from a long line of Nash and Edgecombe County residents. Her great-great-grandfather was Elisha Battle, who settled the area in the 1740s. Her great-grandfather was Turner Westray Battle, captain of the Confederate Guards, a local company in the Civil War. Her grandfather was Jacob

Martha Westray Battle Boyce Long volunteered to serve in the Women's Army Corps (WACs) when World War II began. By the end of the war, she became director of the WACs, the highest ranking woman in the United States Army, and the first woman to earn the Legion of Merit. (United States Army photo from North Carolina Office of Archives and History.)

Battle, state senator and superior court judge. Martha gave up her job in insurance to work in Washington for the National Recovery Administration and the Rural Electrical Administration during the Depression. Then in 1942, she volunteered to join the army. By the end of the war, she became the director of the WACs, the highest woman officer in the U.S. Army. She died in 1972 and in 1998, the state of North Carolina placed a historic marker near her grave in the Battle family graveyard on Highway 97 between Rocky Mount and Tarboro.

In several families, brothers enlisted together. Three sons of Mr. and Mrs. Oscar Farmer of Macclesfield joined the army. Two sons of Jet Webb of Macclesfield also joined the army. Mrs. Lucy Webb of Crisp had four sons in the army; one, Andrew Douglas Webb, was killed in action in North Africa. Three sons of Mrs. Hattie Lewis were in the army and a fourth son was employed in the Baltimore shipyards. Mr. and Mrs. J.D. Phillips had three sons in service: two in the marines and one in the army. Mr. and Mrs. Ellis E. Phillips of Rocky Mount had three sons in the army. The three sons of Mrs. Dilla Ellis of Macclesfield served in the army. Mr. and Mrs. Earl Harper of Pinetops also had three sons in the army.

Wilson Durwood Leggett Jr., the son of Katherine Howard and W.D. Leggett Sr., of Tarboro attended the U.S. Naval Academy. He saw active duty in WW I and WW II, obtaining the rank of Rear Admiral. After the war, he became chief of the navy's Bureau of Ships, the highest engineering post in the U.S. Navy. He was the navy's top expert on internal combustion engines. James Fuller, a graduate of the Pattillo High School class of 1937, attended Tuskeegee Institute and after completing flight training, became a Tuskeegee Airman. He flew 76 combat missions over Europe as part of the first Black air squadron to serve our country.

Many who served were decorated. Captain William D. Gatling and Captain Herbert H. Taylor Jr. won the Silver Star. Staff Sergeant Len Greene of Rocky Mount was awarded the Bronze Star. Staff Sergeant Walter W. Phillips, Staff Sergeant Pheston G. Shelton Jr., and Private First Class Joseph Lewis received the Distinguished Flying Cross for meritorious service. Staff Sergeant George W. Killebrew, Staff Sergeant W.T. Webb, and 2nd Lieutenant Willis E. Cobb were awarded the Air Medal. Guy Alford of Conetoe and Private David Hyde received Purple Hearts.

Charles Gorham Jr. was commissioned through the ROTC and sent to North Africa in 1941. He received the Air Medal for meritorious achievement in aerial flights. First Lieutenant Gorham was killed when his B-29 bomber crashed at Tinker Field, Oklahoma, while attempting an emergency landing on February 9, 1945. Many others didn't make it home either. A total count of those who died in the war from this county is not available, but they include Staff Sergeant Fred W.

Conetoe student 4-H members marched in this community parade in the 1940s down Main Street in Tarboro. (Courtesy of Blount-Bridgers House Archives.)

Walston of Pinetops, Corporal Charles E. Howard Jr. of Macclesfield, Sergeant Johnnie Johnson of Tarboro, Private First Class Med. Det. Milton G. Fussell of Tarboro, and Gaston Gay of Rocky Mount.

Edgecombe County was recognized with the launching of the U.S.S *Edgecombe*, an attack transport ship. The ship was paid for with funds raised in the county through bond drives. The ship remained in service after the war, and its crew requested pictures from local girls to become their pin-up girl. At least four girls submitted photos, and apparently all were so lovely that the crew accepted them all.

Less than a year after the war ended, plans were made to create a special memorial for veterans. Dr. J.G. Raby and the Tarboro Rotary Club proposed that the Edgecombe County Memorial Library be built in honor of its servicemen and women. At the time, the county library was occupying the second floor of the community house, the Blount House, and was short on space. A library committee was formed in September 1946 to raise the funds for a new library, and the Edgecombe County Commissioners pledged $40,000. The Town of Tarboro held a bond drive for another $40,000 and local citizens donated the remaining $40,000. It took almost ten years to complete the library, but the modern brick structure on the corner of Baker and Main Streets finally opened in September 1955.

The U.S.S. Edgecombe, *an attack transport ship, was commissioned in October 1944 with a crew of over 400 men and 40 officers. She sailed from San Francisco to the Pacific in the spring of 1945. She spent almost a week at Okinawa collecting casualties to transport to Pearl Harbor. She was in the Philippines when the war ended. She made several trips transporting troops stateside and was placed in reserve in 1947, after receiving a battle star for her service. (Courtesy of United States Navy, Blount-Bridgers House Archives.)*

The Edgecombe County Memorial Library was built in 1955 at the corner of Main and Baker Streets on the site of the Dr. Baker Home. Prior to this, the library had been located in the Blount-Bridgers House, which served as a community center. (Courtesy of Blount-Bridgers House Archives.)

The headline of the September 30, 1946 *Daily Southerner* announced the first major textile strike in the history of the county: "Hart Mill Union on Strike." Half the employees of that mill walked out, demanding wages 18¢ an hour higher. The mill offered a 7¢ raise, since employees had just received a 29 percent increase in May, when the Textile Workers Union won bargaining rights. The mill then offered an 8¢ addition, for a minimum wage of 73¢ per hour. A union representative refused that offer and it was withdrawn. The workers stayed out a week, but there was no violence during the strike. The final settlement gave employees 70¢ per hour.

Just three years later, Hart Mills was in the news with another strike. In May 1949, Tarboro was the center of attention, as the Textile Workers Union of America began a strike that lasted for months and kept 500 people out of work at Hart Mills. The strike served as a test case for union support in southern states, especially North Carolina. Some workers broke through the picket line and continued to work, causing division within their families. After seven months, the strike ended without the union's demands being met.

Two businesses that opened or expanded in Tarboro remained in business for over 50 years. William Redden "Bill" Long grew up on a farm in eastern Edgecombe County near Lawrence and learned at an early age to repair farm machinery. In 1937, he started his own repair business. His business grew so that by 1940 he was selling equipment as well. In 1941, he moved to Tarboro, hired some men, and built a new office and factory on Main Street. The enterprise sold over $200,000 in its first year. By 1946, Long was manufacturing machinery including the Long Silent Flame Tobacco Curer, the Home Heater, and Floor Furnace. Bill Long was a "born engineer" according to his peers. He designed a hay baler in the late 1940s that sold over 4,000 units. By the 1950s, Long Manufacturing had contracts to produce farm equipment with several major companies, including Ford. Long also produced the first peanut combine and a mechanical tobacco harvester that sold worldwide. The company grew so fast that by the 1960s, there were branches in Iowa, Texas, Pennsylvania, Tennessee, Georgia, and Washington, D.C.

Barnhill Contracting Company was founded in 1949 by Robert E. Barnhill Sr. and his son R.E. Barnhill Jr. Its major contracts included the construction of Interstate 95 in Virginia and North Carolina, Crabtree Office Center in Raleigh, and the four-lane Highway 64 from Tarboro to Rocky Mount.

At mid-century, Edgecombe County had over 51,000 residents. World War II was still fresh in everyone's mind when the Korean conflict began. By the time it ended in 1953, over 1,890 county men and women had been on active duty. Shortly after the Korean War ended in 1953, almost 50 couples in Edgecombe

In 1958, Princeville was flooded for the fourth time in the first half of the twentieth century; the other floods were in 1919, the 1930s, and 1940. (Courtesy of Blount-Bridgers House Archives.)

County received the shocking news that their marriages were not valid: the officiating justice of the peace had inadvertently let his commission expire. The couples had the choice of remarrying or waiting for the general assembly to pass a special law legalizing their marriages.

Natural disasters continued to plague the area. The Tar River flooded Princeville and other areas in 1954 and again in 1958. In that second flood, the National Guard provided food and supplies. The Army Corps of Engineers studied the area and, with the support of congressman L.H. Fountain, a dike was finally built on the Princeville side of the river. The most destructive disaster came in October 1954 when Hurricane Hazel brought death and damage to the entire region. Luther Walters was killed when the storm's high winds blew a tree onto the pack house where he was working. Electrical power was out for several days. An aerial survey of the county indicated that all types of buildings were damaged, from schools to tobacco barns. Three schools in the southern part of the county had their roofs blown off. Store glass windows in Tarboro were blown out. Numerous homes were damaged and streets all over town were blocked by fallen trees.

Baseball continued to provide popular entertainment. Its climate and landscape made North Carolina a popular place for minor league teams. In the 1920s, even smaller towns such as Pinetops, Macclesfield, and Enfield had teams along with the larger towns like Tarboro and Rocky Mount. Tarboro even had farm teams for the Philadelphia As and Baltimore Orioles. The team names reflected the community: the Tars, the Railroaders, the Leafs. Perhaps the most memorable game was played on June 2, 1951. Tarboro, a member of the Coastal Plain League, was playing rival Wilson. In the fifth inning, Wilson used seven pitchers, but could not stop its opponents. Tarboro set team and league records: 24 runs in one inning, 25 batters before an out was scored, and a total of 29 batters in one inning. The final score was Tarboro 31, Wilson 4—truly a game to remember.

Several Edgecombe citizens contributed to the community and the state. Southern Edgecombe County was the birthplace of Lucy Cherry Crisp in 1899. She studied music at the North Carolina College for Women in Greensboro and continued her education at Columbia, Boston, and Radcliffe Colleges. She then taught school and music throughout the state. During the 1930s and 40s, she was a regular columnist for the *News and Observer*. She composed two volumes of poetry: *Spring Fever* in 1935 and *Brief Testament* in 1947. Lucy was a counselor at the University of Illinois and director of the Florence (South Carolina) Museum of Art and History. During WW II, she was director of the USO club in Greenville. A leading advocate for the arts in North Carolina, she was director of the Raleigh Art Museum, which later became the North Carolina Museum of Art. She also helped establish the Greenville Arts Center. Lucy Crisp died in 1977 and was buried in Falkland in Pitt County.

Julia Cherry Spruill (no relation to Lucy Cherry Crisp) was also born in 1899, in Rocky Mount. Her mother was active in the suffragist movement and taught her daughter about women's rights. While in college, Julia participated in the chorus, the literary club, and basketball. Following her mother's lead, Julia taught school in Rocky Mount in the 1920s, until she married Rhodes Scholar Corydon Spruill and moved to Chapel Hill. Her husband was on the faculty at the University of North Carolina and Julia taught at Chapel Hill High School. She attended the master's program as the only woman in the UNC history seminar. In 1938, after ten years of intensive research, she completed *Women's Life and Work in the Southern Colonies*. The tome of Southern women's history became a classic and earned fabulous reviews, including one that praised it as "a model of research and exposition, an important contribution to American Social history to which students will constantly return". The book was published in paperback in 1972 and is still used in today's classrooms. Although she taught part time at UNC until 1949, Julia considered herself a housewife. She died in 1986. A prestigious award in women's history is annually given in her honor by the Southern Association for Women Historians. Her husband left an endowment for the Spruill Chair of Women's History at UNC.

Lawrence H. Fountain, better known as L.H., was a Leggett native who served in the North Carolina senate from 1947 to 1952. A graduate of the University of North Carolina, he earned his J.D. in 1936 and practiced law in Tarboro. During World War II, he served in the Judge Advocate General's office. In 1952, he ran for Congress representing Edgecombe County and the second district of North Carolina. He won reelection for the next 30 years, and for many of those 15 elections, he ran unopposed. For 22 years, Fountain served on the Advisory Commission on Intergovernmental Relations to coordinate programs on the federal, state, and local levels. In 1967, he was appointed by President Johnson as a delegate to the United Nations. He also served on the House Foreign Affairs Committee. For 14 years, Fountain was chairman of the subcommittee on Near Eastern Affairs.

People admired Fountain and what he stood for. He had perfect Sunday school attendance for 80 years, holding classes on planes and trains while he was traveling. He also helped get the dike built on the Princeville side of the Tar River. In 1981, his last term in Congress, his alma mater conferred the honorary degree of Doctor of Laws. After 30 years in Congress, Fountain retired in 1982. In 2001, State Highway 64 between Rocky Mount and Tarboro was named the L.H. Fountain Highway. Edgecombe County lost this remarkable man on October 10, 2002.

6. SOCIAL, EDUCATIONAL, AND INDUSTRIAL CHANGE 1960–1990

The Presidential election, school integration, a census year—all took a back seat to the biggest local story of 1960: Tarboro celebrated its 200th birthday. A special ceremony was held on the town common and a time capsule was buried to be opened at the 300th celebration in 2060. The *Daily Southerner*, which has been in the town for 136 years, produced a special issue dedicated to the history of the county and the town. One feature included histories of many of the small communities, businesses, churches, and schools in the county.

Many of the businesses active in 1960 are gone now: Mizell's Men's Store, Benton Furniture Company, Hart Cotton Mill, Tarboro Coca-Cola Bottling Company, C&W Equipment Company, Rosenbloom-Levy, B&M Chevrolet, Clayton Printing House, Moore's Pharmacy, Shugar's Department Store, Rosenbaum's, Hyman's Ladies Wear, Runnymede Mills, DeBerry's Colonial Dining Room, E.V. Zoeller & Company Druggists, Tarboro Ice and Coal Company, W.S. Clark & Sons Department Store, Robert's Jewelers, Heilig-Meyers, Adler's, and Belk-Tyler. Others are still active over 40 years later: Roberson-Dupree Shoes, Tarboro Home Savings & Loan, Edgecombe-Martin Electric Membership Corporation, Long Manufacturing, Carlisle Funeral Home, Creech the Florist, Piggly Wiggly, Thorne Drug Company, J.E. Simmons Furniture Company, and Henderson Lumber Company.

However, also in 1960, Edgecombe County lost its most ardent patriot, Miss Mattie Shackleford. Originally from Virginia, Miss Mattie began serving Edgecombe County at the beginning of the twentieth century as matron of nurses at Pittman Memorial Hospital. When the hospital closed in 1916 due to lack of funds, she volunteered for military service. She spent two years in France as a nurse. Then she worked for the Serbian Relief Commission. She came back to Tarboro in the 1920s and became director of the County Poor House, which she helped relocate to a new building during the 1930s. She was the only woman to serve as commander of the local American Legion post in 1930–1931. Miss Mattie

In June 1960, Edgecombe County lost Miss Mattie Shackleford, who spent over 40 years in Tarboro taking care of the sick, the old, and the poor. She had been a nurse in World War I. After the war, she became a nurse at Pittman Hospital. Soon, she took over management of the County Poor House, where she lived until her death. She restored the Old Time Cemetery and arranged for the construction of a Memory Chapel there. Her legacy was placed by the many who loved her on this monument by the chapel.

led the county's Memorial Day, Independence Day and Flag Day ceremonies for over 30 years. She built the Memory Chapel in Old Town Cemetery to honor veterans. She also helped restore the Old Town Cemetery that had been neglected and vandalized. She died on June 20, 1960. In addition to the traditional marker placed by her Memory Chapel, her friends inscribed a granite stone with her motto: "What I had, I lost; what I saved, I spent; but what I gave, I have."

New industries came to the county in 1960, when Glenoit began to manufacture rugs and Carolina Enterprise to make plastic toys. Glenoit was one of the successes of the Tarboro Edgecombe Development Corporation, which worked to bring business and industry to the area. Community leaders began to realize that agriculture, while still important, might not provide for the county's economic needs in the future. In 1950, Edgecombe County had almost 4,000 farmers. In just ten years, the number dropped to under 2,700. The cost of special equipment, market trends, and weather had caused many farmers to look for other forms of employment. In another 20 years, fewer than 800 farms were still producing crops. Despite this drop in quantity of farms, production quantity went up. The staple crops were the same as they had been for almost a century: cotton, tobacco, and peanuts. Secondary crops included corn, wheat, and soybeans. In the 1940s and 1950s, farmers averaged 1,000 pounds of tobacco and 400 pounds of cotton per acre. By 1980, fertilizers, crop rotation, and hybrid seeds helped farmers to double their output to 2,300 pounds of tobacco and 740 pounds of cotton per acre.

Its bicentennial led to some changes in downtown Tarboro. Some decided to modernize by demolishing the 70-year-old Town Hall with its town clock, jail, fire department, and opera house. To the horror of many citizens, instead of adding on to the existing structure, the historic building was torn down in 1962 and replaced with a modern plain office building. The next year, plans were made to replace the brick courthouse, also a historic building, which had been built in the 1830s to replace a wooden structure. The courthouse had undergone several additions and modifications over time. Again, some citizens wanted a more modern structure to provide more space, launching the Edgecombe County Historical Society (ECHS). The ECHS would not allow another landmark to be destroyed and replaced with a functional, but boring, structure. To appease the group, an architect designed a building more suitable to the history of the 200-year-old town. Although some expected a Federal-style building reflective of the

The Edgecombe County Courthouse was built in 1835 on the corner of Main and St. James Streets. It was expanded in 1905 and continued to serve the county until being torn down in 1964. A new courthouse was constructed on St. Andrew Street. (Courtesy of Blount-Bridgers House Archives.)

1770s, the new courthouse was modeled after the *c.* 1690s Colonial Williamsburg insane asylum.

The ECHS was founded and supported by many local citizens who had roots in the area for over 100 years. Jaquelin Nash, Arthur Edmondson, Edward U. Lewis and his wife Margaret Battle Lewis, Judge George Britt, Captain Henry Clark Bridgers Jr., Jacquline B. Aycock, Sarah Brinson, Mary Collins Powell, Mary Ferebee Howard, Victor Gray Herring, and Mahlon De Loatch dedicated many hours to preserving or renovating historic structures and bringing recognition to the rich history of Edgecombe County. In October 1969, the group held an open house in the newly-acquired Pender Museum. This edifice was originally the Everett house, built between 1795 and 1810 in the southeastern section of the county near Conetoe. Miss Katherine Pender left a bequest to establish a local history museum as a memorial to her family. The three-room house with its shed addition on the back porch was moved to Tarboro to the lot behind the Blount House. It was used to exhibit items donated to the ECHS. Mrs. Robert W. Scott, wife of the governor, gave the dedication address on October 15, 1969.

In this photo, students leave Tarboro High School at the end of school in the mid-1960s. The school was located at the east end of the town common. (Photo by Skip Wamsley, Tarboro Edgecombe Development Corporation, courtesy of Blount-Bridgers House Archives.)

President Lyndon Johnson visited Edgecombe County in 1864 to launch his war on poverty. Johnson took a train to a farm just outside of Rocky Mount. Governor Terry Sanford joined Johnson on the porch of the William D. Marlow farm house where the President announced to the American public his campaign to end poverty. In a later interview, one of the Marlow children remarked, "we didn't know we were poor until the President told us we were." Although he did not visit the county seat of Tarboro, Johnson was officially the second president to visit Edgecombe.

The *Edgecombe County Chronicle* was published as a weekly for most of 1966. Regular columns included a book review, a music column, and recognition of an outstanding citizen. Penny Bridgers wrote sketches of many who were recognized for contributions to the welfare of the county and were involved in civic programs. John Vines Cobb was a member of the county commissioners and the Edgecombe Welfare Board. He was also a banker, insurance agent, and manager of a cotton warehouse, and was named on May 4, 1966. Alfonso Forbes Felton, also a member of the county commissioners, Mayor of Macclesfield, and a member of the County Board of Education, was recognized on May 18. On May 25, C. Scott Winstead—a WW I veteran who was active in Macclesfield on the Town Board, on the Board of Education, and the Edgecombe County Election board—was honored. He was followed on June 1 by Samuel Burney Kittrell, mayor of Pinetops and a charter member of the Pinetops Lions Club and the Coastal Plains Heart Association. Henry Gray Shelton of Speed was president of the Edgecombe Mutual Livestock Association. He served in the North Carolina Senate from 1956–1962 and also on the Edgecombe County Board of Health and Edgecombe General Hospital Board of Trustees. Shelton was appointed to the State Highway Commission and the State Board of Agriculture, and was profiled on June 8. W.J. "Bill" Eason of Macclesfield, a charter member of the Farm Bureau of Edgecombe County who also served on many community boards, was recognized on June 22. The next week, W.E. Phillips Jr. was commended. Phillips was a charter member of the Pinetops Lions Club and managed the Pinetops Oil Mill, Pinetops Bonded Warehouse, and W.E. Phillips Company. He was mayor of Pinetops for 16 years and served over 24 years with the Pinetops Fire Department. Sam Carlisle of Tarboro was recognized on July 13. He was a charter member of the Tarboro Kiwanis Club, operated an ambulance service for the county, and went into business with his father in Carlisle Funeral Home. Dr. Spencer Bass, a Tarboro native, was educated by Mr. Frank Wilkinson. He studied medicine at the University of Virginia and built a small hospital in Tarboro in 1928. Dr. Bass had an avid interest in history and often wrote features for area papers. He was chairman of the pediatrics section of the North Carolina Medical Association and was featured on July 27.

Two 1966 business announcements signalled more progress for the county. The Anaconda Cable Company opened in the Edgecombe Industrial Park. The North Carolina Highway Department decided that a four-lane route was needed from the capital to the coast. The resulting Route 64 promised to bring tourists and possibly new business to the area.

Edgecombe Technical Institute began as a branch of Wilson Technical Institute in 1968. Within three years, it became a separate facility located on an 82-acre campus on the old county prison site. The college offered one-year training and two-year degrees in business, health, and technical fields. While the oldest building on the campus is the old prison, when Black & Decker came to Tarboro in 1971, a new building was added to train its employees. Soon, an administration and classroom building was added. In 1990, a third building was added to house the library and more classrooms. The college had over 1,000 full-time students in 1977 and its continuing education department served another 4,000.

In 1972, the Edgecombe Technical College opened a branch campus in Rocky Mount in an old store front on Tarboro Street that had been the Rocky Mount Post Office. A new building replaced the storefront in 1988 and was expanded in 1995. Today, Edgecombe Community College has an enrollment of over 2,300 full-time students in computer technology, electronics, and multiple health programs including nursing, radiology, and respiratory therapy, as well as a college transfer program.

The 1954 Supreme Court ruling, *Brown vs. Board of Education*, did not impact Edgecombe County until the 1960s. Since the beginning of the century, Edgecombe had numerous community schools, but the Supreme Court ruled that separate but equal schools were no longer acceptable. The Pearsall Plan developed by the North Carolina General Assembly allowed each school district to decide how and when to integrate its public schools. Edgecombe County allowed students to apply to any schools. Only a small number of African Americans enrolled in what had been all white schools. In the *Charlotte-Mecklenberg* case, the Supreme Court amended its earlier ruling and declared that all public schools must reflect the proportionate population of their communities. The resulting school integration spurred building new schools, closing old community schools, and created integrated consolidated schools. Formerly Black schools were closed or reorganized as middle schools, while white schools often became high schools. The previously Black graded Phillips School became a middle school. North Edgecombe, formerly a white graded, became a high school. Two elementary schools, Coker-Wimberly and Willow Grove, were built to serve the northern part of the county. In the southern part, formerly Black graded Carver became an elementary school and the white graded West Edgecombe became a middle school. Southwest High School opened in 1972 as an integrated campus. Several small private academies also developed in reaction, as white parents chose to remove their children from integrated schools.

Tarboro, then a separate school district, also changed. The all-Black W.A. Pattillo School became an elementary school. The formerly white Tarboro High School became C.B. Martin Middle School, and a new high school was built. Several elementary schools, including Princeville, Stocks, and Bridgers were integrated. Although Edgecombe took 18 years to comply with the original Supreme Court ruling, for the most part, its forced integration was peaceful

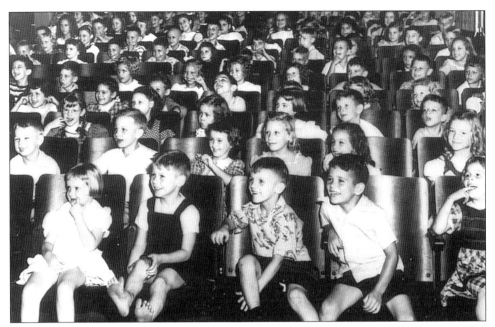

Dozens of elementary school children enjoyed a program at a public school auditorium in the early 1960s, before schools were integrated. (Courtesy of Edgecombe County Memorial Library.)

compared to other places in the state where riots occurred and the police and National Guard had to be summoned.

THE 1970s

The new decade of the 1970s saw even more industry growth. Black & Decker, a national manufacturer of power tools, opened a factory north of Tarboro in 1971. Polylok, a maker of women's apparel and vertical blinds, also employed residents in its new plant. The new Tarboro High School on the corner of Western Boulevard and Howard Avenue stimulated more development in that area. Park Hill Mall became the county's first enclosed mall. The area's first large mall, Tarrytown Mall, had opened in Rocky Mount in 1966. There were also two shopping centers in Tarboro, Fairview on north Main Street near the old fairgrounds, just past the train depot, and the Tarboro Shopping Center on St. Andrew Street. Park Hill Mall became home to Belk-Tyler (which moved from downtown), G.C. Murphy Dime Store, and K-Mart, along with many smaller shops. Eventually, the Colonial Theatre closed downtown and reopened in the mall. A McDonald's also opened on the edge of the mall across from the high school.

One of the most prominent American artists of the twentieth century, Edgecombe County native Hobson Pittman, died in 1972. Born in 1899 in the Epworth community in the eastern part of the county, Pittman revealed his creative

Lydia Gatling Barden and Gene Featherstone perform a duet in the Hobson Pittman Gallery during a special event for visiting legislators. This 1987 meeting marked the bicentennial of their 1787 meeting. (Courtesy of Blount-Bridgers House Archives.)

talent in elementary school. After graduation from Tarboro High School, he attended Columbia University Teachers College and Carnegie Institute. He also studied in Europe as a Guggenheim fellow. Pittman taught for over 40 years at the Philadelphia Museum of Art, the Pennsylvania Academy of Fine Arts, and Pennsylvania State College. His work was featured in major American magazines in the 1940s and 1950s and exhibited in the nation's foremost museums. He received the North Carolina Award in the Fine Arts, the state's highest honor for distinguished service in arts education, in 1968. Pittman's artistic style ranged from still lifes to Southern landscapes of old homes or empty rooms referred to as "The South Remembered." Pittman's niece gave works from his estate to his home town. Tarboro leaders restored the Blount-Bridgers House (as the Blount Community House had been renamed in 1980), turning its second floor into an art gallery honoring Hobson Pittman and displaying local artists and traveling exhibits.

Edgecombe County celebrated the nation's bicentennial in 1976 with a parade, historic pageants, speeches, and recognition of national and local history. Its newspaper also celebrated 150 years of operation. The next year, Tarboro was selected as an All-America City. With a population of only 9,000, Tarboro was the smallest city of the ten winners from over 370 candidates. The official announcement came in November 1976 and brought state attention to the small town. The resulting celebration proved to be larger than the town's bicentennial in 1960. Main Street was decorated with each store having a special All-America display. A parade was held on Saturday, May 14, 1977. The governor honored the town with a special citation and several neighboring cities sent congratulations. The April 20 Raleigh *News & Observer* documented that:

> Tarboro has long been known for the graciousness of its people, the beauty of its homes and for its exceptional Town Common. The town grew up on tobacco, cotton and naval stores derived from the pine forests around it. It has in the past two decades attracted new, modern industry of quality and healthy diversification. And it has, as well, during that same span, moved through racial strife to racial cooperation. It was its recent efforts in housing, voter registration, community development and historical preservation that won for it this deserved honor. Tarboro has accomplished much and has done it while still keeping its basic identity intact. It continues to be, as a Bicentennial advertisement of itself claimed it was, a town of friendly people who live a peaceful and gentle, happy life.

This poster was created in the 1970s for a tour of homes, showing off the historical heritage of the community. (Courtesy of Blount-Bridgers House Archives.)

In the May 13, 1977 Raleigh *News & Observer*, several people were interviewed about what made Tarboro special. Their comments included, "It's the only town I've seen where merchants and businessmen seem to have a sincere desire to serve the people" and, "the community is a wholesome place to live." Mayor Moses Ray revealed:

> We have been able to face our problems and work for the solutions without the riots, the bombings and the beatings that have occurred in so many towns around us. I'm not saying Tarboro is a utopia. We still have problems – the All America City thing wasn't given to us because we had solved all our problems—but we're facing them.

Mayor Ray was an African-American dentist who had served on the Tarboro Town Council for 12 years. He was also a leader of the East Tarboro Citizens League, a Black community development group. The League had been active since 1963, working to improve voter registration among African Americans and provide employment opportunities, better housing, and recreational equipment.

The Tarboro Edgecombe Development Corporation (TEDCO) formed in 1958. Under the leadership of Peyton Beery, the agency worked hard to recruit industry and business. By the time of the All-American recognition, Tarboro had "four automobile dealerships, a string of regional department stores, two active shopping

The E.L. Roberson Center on Albemarle Avenue opened on July 1, 1977. The center is operated by the Town of Tarboro and offers programs for senior citizens. It features a game room, an arts and crafts area, a library, and a dining room.

Martin Middle School band students performed for the annual Happening on the Common, a festival held each May on the town common that features food, entertainment, and rides. (Photo by Peyton Berry, courtesy of Blount-Bridgers House Archives.)

centers and a buzzing central business district." The county also had 18 major industries manufacturing such items as communication cable, power tools, a variety of textiles, plastic toys, buttons, mattresses, caskets, rugs, seatbelts, and farm machinery. Another successful venture of TEDCO was Hendricks Park Urban Renewal Project on Albemarle Avenue, which resulted in new housing and the E.L. Roberson Center. In 1978, TEDCO helped recruit another new industry, Edmont (now Ansell-Edmont), which manufactured industrial-grade rubber gloves.

The school system in 1977 was separated into county and city districts. The Tarboro School system had 3,000 students spread amongst one high school, located in a fairly new facility on the corner of Western Boulevard and Howard Avenue; one middle school, C.B. Martin; and four elementary schools. Edgecombe County had ten schools to serve 7,000 students.

In 1977, the National Parks Service designated a 45-block area of Tarboro as a Historic District and a National Recreation Trail. This historic district is one of the largest in the state and features architecture from the 1790s through the 1930s. Three years later, Tarboro was selected to be part of the Main Street USA program. This distinction brought grants to restore existing buildings and revitalize the downtown business district.

THE 1980s

Like the previous decade, the eighties continued to be a time of growth and surprises from mother nature. The county population increased about 3,000 from the last census, with 55,998 citizens. Approximately 1,000 residents were added to Tarboro, bringing its population to over 9,400. Rocky Mount, in both Nash and Edgecombe Counties, had over 41,000 people.

As the population grew, several public programs and services were created or expanded. In 1982, the Blount-Bridgers House opened officially as a history museum and art gallery. In 1983, the library established a branch in Pinetops. Two years later, Edgecombe County Memorial Library opened an 11,243-square-foot addition, part of which was dedicated as the Janie F. Allsbrook Local History Room in 1986 in honor of the long-time county librarian who served from 1941–1970. Also in 1985, Heritage Hospital replaced the outdated Edgecombe General. The Albemarle opened as a retirement community in the spring of 1983. Its 150 residential apartments house retirees from North Carolina (when it first opened, Edgecombe County natives were only a third of the residents) and other states including Florida, Virginia, Maryland, and New York. The facility offered a fine dining room, an activity center with a baby grand piano for concerts and local programs, and a small chapel featuring a stained glass window from the Jewish synagogue that had been torn down in the 1970s.

*The new Heritage Hospital opened in 1985 with superior medical technology over the old Edgecombe General Hospital. By 1990, the hospital offered helicopter service to Pitt Memorial Regional Hospital in Greenville. (*Daily Southerner *photo collection, courtesy of Edgecombe County Memorial Library.)*

Princeville celebrated its 100th birthday in 1985. The town had a birthday party and was featured on area television programs. While much of the community consisted of elderly residents who had been born there, some young people attended schools and encouraged growth. Then the town experienced some serious problems due to poor town management. Eventually, the Local Government Commission of the North Carolina Department of the Treasury stepped in to reorganize the town government. With new leadership, Princeville residents explored ways of improving the town and promoting its heritage. By the late 1990s, grants and other programs were stimulating the local economy.

Downtown Tarboro experienced new ventures. Mary Ann Holderness opened Rusty's Unique Gifts in a refurbished store on Main Street in 1982. Sammy Harrell opened Sammy's Men Shop after W.S. Clark's department store closed in 1980. Rusty Holderness helped organize several small merchants into a renovated Clark building known as Clark Square, a sort of mini-mall on Main Street that included Sammy's, Peter Pan children's clothing store, Paperworks card and gift shop, Unicorn Books, and Tarboro Antiques. The specialty shops at Clark Square and other downtown businesses strove to meet the needs of area residents. Tom and Patsy Miller welcomed tourists into their Little Warren Bed and Breakfast beginning in 1985, and other residents in the historic district also opened inns or bed and breakfasts. The following year, the acting bug bit a few locals when a Hollywood crew filmed a movie in the area.

Consolidated Diesel Company built a plant near Whitakers in 1983 and employed over 300 in the production of engines. In the last year of the decade, Edgecombe County put a central communication center for police/fire/emergency into operation. Concerned citizens established Edgecombe Hospice to assist the terminally ill and their families in that year as well. And Sara Lee, a national bakery, opened a facility in Edgecombe County south of Tarboro, employing several hundred.

The largest snowfall in the history of the state fell on March 1, 1980, delivering over 18 inches of snow with drifts up to 3 feet. Hundreds of stranded motorists had to take shelter in the National Guard Armory. Schools and some businesses were closed for a week. In 1984 and again in 1988, the area was hit by damaging tornados, earning North Carolina the nickname "Tornado Ally." The 1984 storms killed people throughout the state, but there were no local fatalities—only damage to structures and trees. The 1988 tornado, however, killed two people in neighboring Nash County. The last month of the decade delivered more unusual weather. On December 9th, 1989, Edgecombe experienced a severe ice storm that knocked trees into power lines. Some parts of the county were without power for a week while nighttime temperatures dipped below freezing. Then the weather warmed to the usual December range of the 40 to 50 degrees, but on Christmas Eve, Edgecombe experienced its first white Christmas day in nearly a century.

7. Economic Turmoil and Natural Disaster 1990–2000

The future seemed bright for Edgecombe County and its towns and communities at the dawn of the new decade. The county population had increased by another 1,000 and Tarboro had gained almost 2,000 residents. Housing was expanding in Pinetops, western Tarboro, and several rural communities. In the late 1990s, some communities—such as Speed, Battleboro, Leggett, Macclesfield, and Whitaker—declined in population. Other areas grew: Rocky Mount went from 34,284 in 1970 to almost 50,000 in 1990. Princeville went from 600 to almost 1,600 and Pinetops saw a small growth from 1,379 to over 1,500 from 1970 to 1990.

In 1992, Edgecombe helped send an African American to Congress, representing the district that George White had served almost 100 years earlier. Representative Eva Clayton was also the first woman elected to Congress from North Carolina. Edgecombe Technical Institute had become Edgecombe Community College and opened a new library and classroom building on the Tarboro campus. Main Street Inn Bed and Breakfast opened in the historic Morris House across from the library, luring more tourists to the area.

The Tarboro and Edgecombe County school systems merged quietly and met no resistance—unlike neighboring Nash County, which had an ugly public conflict with the Rocky Mount School system that dragged on for years. Three magnet schools were created: Princeville became a Montessori school and Phillips Middle and North Edgecombe became math/science schools.

The first sign of economic trouble came in October 1990, when Hardee's, a major fast food corporation located in Rocky Mount, laid off 125 of over 1,000 employees at their home office. Then in January 1991, Carolina Telephone—a company that had been in Tarboro for almost 100 years—announced its reorganization would move 400 employees and their families to Wake Forest, a town north of Raleigh about 50 miles west of Tarboro. At the time, Edgecombe County already had an unemployment rate of 5.8 percent. Thus, families left the

In 1994, local artist Susan Fecho worked with area school students to produce a multi-panel mural on the history of the county featuring crops, homes, and historic people. (Courtesy of Blount-Bridgers House Archives.)

local schools, churches, and civic groups and within three years, most had relocated to northern Wake County. However, a few families had other ties to the area and chose not to move. The phone company hired a charter bus to transport employees back and forth to the new offices.

Black & Decker, which had opened a power tool plant in 1971, relocated in 1995, putting 800 people out of work. Other local plants closed and moved to Mexico as part of the North America Free Trade Agreement (NAFTA). In 1996, Rocky Mount Mills closed after operating for 175 years. The unemployment rate in Edgecombe County reached 13 percent, one of the highest in the state. All of the stores that had opened in Clark's Square closed, as many of their customers had moved or were out of work.

In 1996, a meat-processing industry appeared ready to build a new facility in the county. Although some, including many county leaders, saw this as a way to reduce unemployment, others felt this particular industry would be detrimental to the environment. Heated public debates, investigative trips to other plants owned by the parent company in the midwest, and numerous media reports resulted in the county commissioners rejecting the proposal. Efforts were made to recruit other more positive industries to the area.

Mother nature added to the economic problems in September 1996 with Hurricane Fran. Although the storm did not bring much rain, winds of over 100 miles per hour felled trees in the eastern third of the state and left thousands without electricity. The worst damage was around Raleigh, but there was enough damage locally to create a serious respect for hurricanes. Old timers remembered Hurricane Hazel in 1954, but younger people who had not been born then, were particularly frightened by Fran. However, as soon as trees were cleared from the roadways, life quickly returned to normal.

The Edgecombe County Historical Society—so active in the 1960s—had dissolved in the 1980s, as many members died or moved away. A rallying effort was made in the fall of 1997 to save part of the railroad depot complex that was threatened by development. The train depot itself, built in the 1880s, had been closed in the 1970s and sat empty until 1996. It was then torn down without notice from CSX Railroad, owners of the property. CSX wanted such a high price for the corner that those interested in saving the property could not afford to buy it. A developer purchased part of the property and planned to put up a drug store, demolishing the 113-year-old warehouse. Despite pleas from the hastily-reformed Edgecombe Historical Society to renovate the structure into the new store or otherwise save it, it was bulldozed on November 13, 1997.

Edgecombe County made the national news when General Henry Hugh Shelton was appointed Chairman of the Joint Chiefs of Staff of the United States Military by President Clinton on October 1, 1997. Once again, an Edgecombe resident was a significant leader in the national military. Shelton, a native of Speed, is the son of Sarah Laughlin and the late Hugh Shelton. He attended North Edgecombe School before graduating from N.C. State. In 1991, he was promoted to major general and commanded the 82nd Airborne Division at Fort Bragg, North Carolina. Shelton attended both ranger and airborne schools and completed a special forces course before serving two terms in Vietnam. Shelton was an "A" DELTA team commander and served with the 101st in Operation Desert Shield and Operation Desert Storm. He was awarded the Defense Distinguished Service Medal, Legion of Merit, Bronze Star with Valor, Purple Heart, Meritorious Service Medal, and Army Commendation Medal. He has also provided tremendous service to his home state. He was honored with the 4-H Lifetime Achievement Award from the North Carolina 4-H Youth Development program. In 1999, Governor Hunt awarded him the Order of the Long Leaf Pine, the highest award given by the state. After his retirement, Congress gave him the Congressional Gold Medal in September 2002. Shelton is married to the former Carolyn Johnson, also of Speed.

History was in the headlines again that year when a local firm, Coastal Carolina Research, discovered the remains of one of the earliest settlements in North Carolina along the Chowan River. Loretta Lautzenheiser, owner of the archaeology research firm, was excited about surveying the home of Governor

Charles Eden, which dated to about 1660. Assisting Coastal Carolina Research was Tarboro resident Jaquelin Drane Nash. Mrs. Nash was born in Charlotte and graduated from St. Mary's College in Raleigh in 1930. She met and married Pembroke Nash, son of S.S. Nash, and moved to Tarboro in 1931. She immediately became active in Calvary Episcopal Church and served for 50 years on the Altar Guild. She became the church historian and was the first archivist of the parish. She published her first history, *A Goodly Heritage*, in 1960. She was also active with the Episcopal Church Women and was appointed to the Bishop's Committee for Diocesan Archives and History from 1972–1983.

Mrs. Nash also had a strong interest in the history of Tarboro and its surrounding communities. She spoke to many civic groups about the area's history. She was a member of the North Caroliniana Society and the National Society of the Colonial Dames of America, holding several offices on the state and national levels of the latter group. She spent several terms on the Edenton Historical Commission (making her a valuable assistant in researching the documents to coordinate with the artifacts found by Coastal Carolina Research). She was a founding member and the historian of the Edgecombe County Historical Society. Mrs. Nash served on the Blount-Bridgers House Advisory Committee and on the Tarboro Historic District Commission and was a charter

In May 1999, Edgecombe County honored native son General Henry Hugh Shelton, chairman of the Joint Chiefs of Staff, with a reception at Edgecombe Community College Campus. Goernor James B. Hunt presented General Shelton with the Order of the Long Leaf Pine, the highest honor paid to a state resident.

On September 15, 1999, Hurricane Floyd became the second hurricane in a week to dump heavy rains on eastern North Carolina. Several feet of flood waters enveloped the historic Primitive Baptist Church, on the corner of St. James Street and Albemarle Avenue, and the Amoco service station located behind the church.

member of the Tarboro Women's Club. She published articles in several magazines, notably the *State Magazine*, and *NC Garden Club Magazine*. Fourteen of the biographies in the *Dictionary of North Carolina Biography* were written by Mrs. Nash. This remarkable woman "retired" with her husband to the Albemarle, but came out of retirement to conduct some of the research for the Eden House project. She remains Tarboro's "Grand Dame" and its own historical treasure.

The building of a new drugstore and two new hotels (Holiday Inn Express and Comfort Inn) in 1998 seemed to signal that Edgecombe County was emerging from rough economic times. Carolina Systems Technology, a subsidiary of a Japanese auto manufacturer, opened a new plant on McNair Road near Edgecombe Community College. The company makes electronic components for cars and employees over 300 workers. Air Systems Components used the empty Black & Decker plant to create a new firm that made fan boxes and registers for heating and air conditioning units. Another new firm was Catalina Boats. Barnhill Contracting Company was busy working on a new county jail and law enforcement center scheduled to open in 1999. Hurricane Bonnie drenched the area in the fall of 1998, but did not effect the positive attitude of the county residents.

FLOYD AND THE FLOOD OF THE CENTURY

Meteorologists warned North Carolinians that Hurricane Dennis was a potential threat to the state's coast. The area had been so dry that sand bars dotted the Tar River. Dennis was not seen as an inland threat. For a week, the storm hovered on the northeast coast along the Outer Banks drenching the area with over 10 inches of rain and saturating the land. The storm went out to sea and then came back as a weakened tropical storm on September 10, 1999.

Less than a week later, another storm was forecasted. Floyd was bigger and stronger than Dennis. Residents all over eastern North Carolina gathered supplies to prepare for the hurricane, not knowing exactly where it would make land fall. Schools and businesses closed early so most people were home. The storm came ashore south of New Bern on Wednesday, September 15. The category-three storm raged most of Wednesday evening, with the worst coming about midnight. The howling 75-mile-per-hour wind brought down trees and the heavy rains caused flash flooding. Tarboro's power went out during the night. By early afternoon Thursday, the storm had blown away after dumping over 20 inches of rain in less than 24 hours.

Thursday afternoon, September 16, residents surveyed the damage. Trees blocked the streets so driving anywhere was difficult. The town common alone had over two dozen trees down. Along with felled trees, the historic district received some structural damage. One house on Albemarle Avenue was moved

On the afternoon of September 16, the skies cleared so residents could examine the storm damage, such as this downed tree on St. Patrick Street.

completely off its foundation. Power and water were still out, but preliminary radio reports indicated no serious injuries. Residents believed the worst was over, and some who had evacuated to shelters or relatives even returned home. They used cell phones and car phones to contact friends and family. Little did they know that early Friday morning, the terror would begin anew and it would be days before the full extent of damage was understood.

The 20 inches of rain from Floyd—added to the 10 inches of Dennis the previous week—could not be held by the streams, creeks, and rivers. They all overflowed their banks and the water kept rising as rumors of a flood began to spread. Owners who could get to their stores began to move stock and sandbag. No flood had ever reached past Granville Street, just two blocks from the river on the Tarboro side. With a dike built at 38 feet (5 feet above the highest recorded flood of 1919), there had not been a flood since 1958 in Princeville. Radio reports indicated that much of Rocky Mount along Stony Creek, which flowed into the Tar River, was flooded. Tarrytown Mall and Lowe's Home Improvement Warehouse were under water. Highway 301 south of Carolina East Mall was not passable, due to high water that stretched up Sunset Avenue and engulfed a major business section of Rocky Mount. As Rocky Mount was upriver, it was clear that the flooding would soon reach Tarboro and other points downriver.

On the afternoon of Friday, September 17, employees in the Register of Deeds office carried records up three flights of stairs in the courthouse. Because the courthouse and the county office building were threatened with rising water, an

Cotton's Restaurant (far right) and Edward D. Jones Financial Office, located at the corner of St. James and Trade Streets, were completely flooded by still-rising waters on the morning of September 18. Both businesses were rebuilt after the flood.

Caro Edmondson's store was a landmark in Old Sparta for over 100 years. It served as a post office for the community as well as a general store. It was destroyed by the 1999 flood. (Courtesy of North Carolina Office of Archives and History.)

emergency center was set up at the newly-opened county jail on Anaconda Road, far away from the rising river.

Members of the Calvary Church choir were summoned to the church Friday afternoon, for a wedding originally scheduled for Saturday. By 4 p.m., they had to wade to the churchyard in knee-deep water. The bride and groom stood in rolled-up jeans in a church illuminated only by candlelight. The bride's parents were not able to get to Tarboro from Leggett, as Bell's Bridge was already underwater. Lane Anderson was given in marriage to Bret Taylor by her parents over a cell phone. It was months before this congregation and many other could return to their churches to worship.

Water and power were still out. Phone calls from people outside the storm area relayed television reports to those trapped in the county. By Friday night, many islands of high ground were accessible only by boat. In the middle of the night, helicopters started retrieving people in Princeville, Contoe, and other places south of Tarboro from their rooftops and transporting them to Tarboro High School. When Saturday morning dawned, the water not only surrounded the town, but covered much of Main Street for five blocks from the river. A couple paddled a canoe down the thoroughfare to check on stores and apartments. Using binoculars, citizens could see only rising water around the Tar River Bridge: the bridge itself—standing 42 feet above the river—was under water. A house appeared to be floating over the road.

The helicopter rescue missions continued for two and half days. By Sunday night, over 3,000 were in the emergency shelter at Tarboro High School. Another

3,500 were in other shelters in the county, most located in schools. Air traffic was so heavy with army, navy, coast guard, and Red Cross helicopters, that the military sent a C-130 air transport to direct the air traffic. Fortunately, three major military bases were located in eastern North Carolina, and the marines literally came to the rescue by providing equipment and supplies. The Fountains of the Albemarle Retirement Center was evacuated and its elderly residents were relocated to temporary shelter at the Moose Lodge. News trucks from CNN, ABC, NBC and CBS all invaded the town. Hurricane Hazel had been "the storm" for over 45 years, but from that point forward, everything was measured by Floyd.

Sunday night, electricity was restored to part of Tarboro. Much of the county, especially to the east and south, was still without power. The new offices of Edgecombe-Martin Electric Co-op were under water, along with many of their trucks. Many streets in Tarboro were washed out by the creeks that ran through town. St. James Street, just east of Albemarle, was washed away by Hendricks Creek. Wilson Street near the Hilma golf course was gone. Pearl Street behind Greenwood Cemetery was also washed out. It was impossible to drive north out of Tarboro because Bell's Bridge was under water. It was also difficult to find a clear route west to Rocky Mount, as many side roads were blocked by fallen trees or high water. It was futile to drive south along Highway 33 towards Greenville, as that area was completely covered. Forty percent of Tarboro was under water. Fishing Creek deluged the town of Speed. Every building in Old Sparta was flooded.

The devastation witnessed on the news or in person was shocking. Images from planes and helicopters showed much of the county underwater. Nothing but rooftops were visible in Princeville or east Tarboro. Although many stories circulated about the Princeville dike breaking, the water actually went around or over the dike into town. The dike was not high enough to keep the water out, but it did hold the water *in* Princeville for over a week.

Although there were many encouraging rescues, losses were almost inconceivable. A family in the Bynum Park area near Pinetops drowned when their boat capsized. Ben Mayo, 50; his wife Vivian, 45; and their daughter Keisha, 24; along with Destiny Flowers, 3; and Cabrina Flowers, 5, were lost. Otis Reid of Pinetops died when water engulfed his mobile home. Two people in Nash County died trying to drive through high water. A number of coffins were washed out of area cemeteries, leaving a disturbing sight. Eventually, these caskets were recovered and the bodies identified and reburied.

Many of the rescue victims were forced to leave their pets behind in the rising water. Once all the people had been rescued, beginning on Monday afternoon, September 20, another group of volunteers took boats and canoes to rescue stranded animals. With help from the Animal Planet rescue team and several area humane society volunteers, over 200 animals (mostly dogs and cats, but also an emu) were transported to the veterinary school at North Carolina State University in Raleigh. By the end of the second week, 400 dogs and cats had been treated and photographed for identification. Many other animals, however, could not be saved: 300 cows, 20 horses, 50 goats and over 1,000 hogs all drowned.

On Monday, September 20, President Bill Clinton stood at the edge of the flood waters at the intersection of Main and Church Streets in Tarboro. Along with Congresswoman Eva Clayton and Governor Jim Hunt, President Clinton promised the people that they would be helped. Power was restored to most homes, but it was over a week before residents had running water. Even then, they were told not to drink it, but to use it for bathrooms only.

Officials were not prepared for the extent of the damages they discovered once they were able to survey the area. Princeville Montessori School and Pattillo Elementary in Tarboro were both covered in over 9 feet of water. Everything was a total loss—furniture, libraries, records. Churches throughout the county were damaged beyond repair. Howard Memorial Presbyterian had over half a million dollars in damage. Calvary Church had to rebuild its fellowship hall and repair its small chapel. The Eastern Star Baptist Church in east Tarboro had to be destroyed, as did St. Paul A.M.E. Zion Church in Tarboro and St. Luke's Church of Christ, Macedonia Church, and the A.M.E. Zion Church in Princeville. St. Stephen's Baptist and the Primitive Baptist, both near the river, were damaged but

On September 20, 1999, President Bill Clinton and FEMA Director James Lee Witt (right) met with Tarboro Mayor Donald Morris beside the police department. President Clinton addressed the community and the nation with a promise of help. In the national broadcast, President Clinton was standing on the corner of Main and Church Streets with a flooded town behind him. (Official White House photograph courtesy of Mayor Donald Morris.)

repaired. In Edgecombe County, over 3,400 homes were damaged. Dozens of businesses were so severely damaged that they never reopened.

Financial statistics alone cannot tell the whole story of the flood. Over $272,000 in livestock and over $47 million in crop damage were reported by the Edgecombe County Agriculture Extension Service. Over $1 billion in disaster relief was designated for this county to repair or replace the thousands of homes and businesses that were damaged.

Schools remained closed until October, as many remained in use as shelters. The community college and several empty stores were set up as distribution centers for the hundreds of truckloads of goods that came into the area from across the county. Hundreds of FEMA trailers where brought in and set in three county parks to provide shelter for those who lost their homes and had nowhere else to go. Most residents moved out of these temporary trailers as soon as apartments or homes were repaired. One lone holdout stayed past the deadline, refusing to give up her trailer until October 2002. The Edgecombe County schools reopened on October 4th. Mobile units were brought in to Stocks Elementary and to Martin Middle to house the students that had been at Pattillo and Princeville. Because a new wing at Princeville was under construction, that school was reopened in 2000. Pattillo students did not get to their new school until the spring of 2002.

Area churches that were not damaged opened their doors to the communicants of displaced congregations. The Tarboro Church of Christ on Daniel Street—with a membership of only 100—welcomed the much larger assembly of St. Luke's Church of Christ in Princeville. The two congregations, one white and one black, held joint services in the Tarboro sanctuary for over a year, while St. Luke's was being rebuilt. They shared Thanksgiving and Christmas services. They had a wonderful vacation bible school the next summer. When St. Luke's was rededicated in the fall of 2001, the guests of honor were the members of the Tarboro church. People from both groups, who knew little or nothing about the other before the flood—formed new friendships.

For almost two years after the flood, volunteers from the Menonite, the Methodist, and the Baptist churches throughout the nation came to Edgecombe County to help tear down and rebuild homes and churches. College students from Pennsylvania and other states gave up their vacations to help strangers in need. Thousands of toys were sent to Tarboro for Christmas in 1999, so its children would not go without. Countless truckloads of clothes, food, and supplies came not only from other North Carolina communities, but from around the world. This outpouring of support helped strengthen the area residents who had suffered losses. Residents helped neighbors and strangers alike, in whatever ways they could. Friends offered their homes as shelter for those who had lost theirs. Before the flood, the Tar River was more than just a physical and social divider between Tarboro and Princeville. After, citizens on both sides worked together to rebuild their communities.

BIBLIOGRAPHY

BOOKS

Barrett, John G. *The Civil War in North Carolina*. Chapel Hill, NC: University of North Carolina Press, 1963.

Battle, Kemp Plummer. *Memories of an Old-Time Tar-Heel*. Chapel Hill, NC: University of North Carolina Press, 1945.

Battle, Herbert, Lois Yelverton and William J. Battle, *The Battle Book: A Genealogy of the Battle Family in America*. Montgomery, AL: Paragon Press, 1930.

Bridgers, Henry Clark, Jr. *East Carolina Railway: Route of the Yellow Hammer*. Tarboro, NC: T&E Publisher of Louisville, Carolina Division, 1973.

———. *The Story of Banking in Tarboro*. Tarboro: Edgecombe Bank and Trust Company, 1969.

Chapman, Craig S. *More Terrible Than Victory: North Carolina's Bloody Bethel Regmient, 1861–1865*. Washington, DC: Brassey, 1993.

Cheshire, Joseph Blount. *Nonnulla: Memories, Stories, Traditions*. Chapel Hill, NC: UNC Press, 1930.

Cobb, E. Tunney, Jr. "Race Relations in Edgecombe County, North Carolina, 1700–1975." unpublished honors thesis: University of North Carolina, 1975.

Cooper, Alonzo. *In and Out of Rebel Prisons*. 1888. rpt. Time-Life Civil War Reprint Library. 1983.

Crabtree, Beth G. and James W. Patton, eds. *Journal of a Secesh Lady: The Diary of Catherine Ann Devereaux Edmondston, 1860–1866*. Raleigh, NC: Division of Archives and History, 1979.

Day, W.A. *A True History of Company I, 49th Regiment North Carolina Troops*. Newton, NC: Enterprise, 1893. RPT Butternut and Blue, 1997.

Edward, Charles. *The Hell You Say*. Raleigh, NC: Old Sparta Press, 1980.

Fleming, Monika. *Images of America: Echoes of Edgecombe County*. Charleston, SC: Arcadia Publishing, 1996.

———. *Images of America: Edgecombe County, Vol. II*. Charleston, SC: Arcadia, 1997.

Hasseler, William, ed. *The General to His Lady: The Civil War Letters of William Dorsey Pender to Fanny Pender*. Chapel Hill, NC: UNC Press, 1962.

Hoffman, Margaret. *The Granville District of North Carolina 1748–1763. Abstracts of Land Grants*. 3 vols. Roanoke Rapids, VA: Roanoke News Company, 1986.

Jenkins, Sara, ed. *The Edgecombe Story.* Tarboro, NC: Edgecombe County Bicentennial Commission, 1976.

Jones, Harry Allen, Jr. *Tarborough and Its Academies,* Greenville, NC: Era Press, 1975.

Justesen, Benjamin. *George Henry White: An Even Chance in the Race of Life.* Baton Rouge, LA: Louisiana State University Press, 2001.

Lichtenstein, Gaston. "Reminiscent, Biographical and Genealogical" in *George Washington's Lost Birthday.* Richmond, VA: Capitol Printing Company, 1924.

———. "Early Tarboro History" in *Thomas Jefferson as War Governor.* Richmond, VA: William Byrd Press, 1925.

Merrens, Harry R. *Colonial North Carolina in the Eighteenth Century.* Chapel Hill, NC: University of North Carolina Press, 1964.

Minchin, Timothy J. *What Do We Need a Union For? The TWUA in the South 1945–1955.* Chapel Hill, NC: University of North Carolina Press, 1997.

Nash, Jaquelin. *A Goodly Heritage: The Story of Calvary Parish.* Tarboro, NC: Colony Episcopal Church, 1960.

———. *In This Holy House: The Story of Grace Memorial Chapel in Lawrence, NC.* Tarboro, NC: n.p., 1994.

Powell, William. *North Carolina Through Four Centuries.* Chapel Hill, NC: University of North Carolina Press, 1985.

Powell, William, ed. *Dictionary of North Carolina Biography.* 6 vols. Chapel Hill, NC: University of North Carolina Press, 1979–1996.

Reason, Betty and Eunice Taylor. *The History of Crisp, NC: Then and Now.* n.p.: 1999.

Reason, Betty, Vera Stallings, and Patricia Keel. *The History of Macclesfield, NC: The First Hundred Years.* Macclesfield, NC: n.p., 2000.

Saunders, William L., ed. *Colonial Records of North Carolina.* 12 vols. Raleigh, NC: Secretary of State's Office, 1886.

Smith, Margaret and Emily Wilson. *North Carolina Women Making History.* Chapel Hill: UNC Press, 1999.

Taylor, Michael W. *To Drive the Enemy from Southern Soil: The Letters of Col. Francis Marion Parker and the History of the 30th Regiment North Carolina Troops.* Dayton, Ohio: Morningside House, 1998.

Taylor, Roland, ed. *Mabrey Bass's Tarboro from 1950 to 1990.* Fuquay-Varina, NC: Research Triangle Publishing, 1997.

Thorpe, John H. *Roster of Nash County Confederate Soldiers and Copy of the Edgecombe County Roster.* Raleigh, NC: Edwards & Broughton, 1925.

Trotter, William R. *Ironclads and Columbiads: The Civil War in North Carolina The Coast.* Winston-Salem, NC: Blair Publishers, 1989.

Turner, J. Kelly and John L. Bridgers, Jr. *History of Edgecombe County, North Carolina.* Raleigh: Edwards & Broughton Printing Co., 1920.

Walters, Ralf. *Hurricane Floyd and the Flood of the Century: Sept. 1999.* Tarboro, NC: *Daily Southerner,* 2000.

Watson, Alan D. *Edgecombe County: A Brief History.* Raleigh, NC: Division of

Archives and History, 1979.

———. *Society in Colonial North Carolina.* Raleigh, NC: Division of Archives and History, 1996.

———. *Society in Early North Carolina: A Documentary History.* Raleigh, NC: Division of Archives and History, 2000.

ARTICLES

Balanoff, Elizabeth. "Negro Legislators in the North Carolina General Assembly July 1868–Feb. 1872." *North Carolina Historical Review.* 49 (1972) 22–55.

Battle, Jeremiah. "Edgecombe County 1811" in the series "Twelve North Carolina Counties 1810–1811" ed. A.R. Newsome. *North Carolina Historical Review.* (1933) 68-99.

Bushong, William B. "William Percival, An English Architect in the Old North State, 1857–1860." *North Carolina Historical Review.* 57 (1980) 310–339.

Cheshire, Mrs. Godfrey. "The Long Days of her Life- A Remarkable Woman: Katharine Drane Cheshire". *The Communicant* 89.5 (July 1998) p. 5.

Foster, Gaines M. "Bishop Cheshire and Black Participation in the Episcopal Church." *North Carolina Historical Review.* 54 (1977) 49–65.

Gass, W. Canard. "A Felicitous Life: Lucy Martin Battle 1805–1874" *North Carolina Historical Review.* 52 (1972) 367–393.

Gebel, Carol W. "The Cool Spring Quilts: A Mid-Nineteenth Century Collection."*North Carolina Humanities.* 2.2 (Spring/Summer 1994) 79–87.

Mobley, Joe. "In the Shadow of White Society: Princeville, A Black Town in North Carolina 1865–1915. *North Carolina Historical Review.* 63 (1986) 340–384.

Norris, David. "The Yankees Have Been Here! The Story of Brig. Gen. Edward E. Potter's Raid on Greenville, Tarboro, and Rocky Mount, July 19–23. 1863." *North Carolina Historical Review* Jan. 1996: 1–27.

Samito, Christian G. "'Patriot by Nature, Christian by Faith': Major General William Dorsey Pender, C.S.A." *North Carolina Historical Review.* 66.2 (April 1999): 163–201.

Steelman, Lela Carr. "The Life-Style of an Eastern North Carolina Planter: Elias Carr of Bracebridge Hall." *North Carolina Historical Review.* 57 (January 1980). 17–42.

Watson, Alan D. "Orphanage in Colonial North Carolina: Edgecombe County as a Case Study." *North Carolina Historical Review*. 52.2 (April 1975) 105–119.

———."Society and Economy in Colonial Edgecombe County." *North Carolina Historical Review*. 50 (Summer 1973): 231–255.

Watson, Helen. "Journalistic Medley: Newspapers and Periodicals in A Small North Carolina Community, 1859–1860." *North Carolina Historical Review*. 60.4 (October 1963) 457–485.

———. "The Books they Left: Some 'Liberies' in Edgecombe County, 1733–1783" North Carolina Historical Review. *48 (*1971), 245–257.

NEWSPAPERS

The Tarboro Free Press
The Tarboro Southerner
The Carolina Banner
The Farmer's Advocate
The Daily Southerner
Edgecombe County Chronicles
The Rocky Mount Telegram
Home Front News

PRIMARY SOURCES

Anderson, Blanche Moore. "Military Record of Confederate Veterans Living in Edgecombe County. 1903." Notebook part of the manuscript collection of Edgecombe Community College Library, Tarboro campus.

Bell, Eugenia. Letter to Eleanor Page, 1832, in the Ross Papers. North Carolina Office of Archives and History.

Brown, Bertram. "UDC Scrapbook of the Reunion of Gettysburg Veterans after attending the July 1913 Event." Edgecombe County Memorial Library Manuscript Collection. Tarboro, NC.

Cheshire, Joseph Blount, Jr.. *Some Account of My Life for my Children.* Unpublished manuscript on microfilm North Carolina Office of Archives and History.

Edgecombe County North Carolina: Her People and Resources. The Foremost Agricultural Section of the State. Raleigh: Broughton Power Printers, 1891. (Original belonging to Captain. H.C. Bridgers Jr. is in the Blount-Bridgers House library.)

McIver, J.A. *Tarboro Baptist Church Year Book and Directory.* Tarboro, NC 1930.

Philips, James J. Papers. Southern History Collection, University of North Carolina at Chapel Hill.

State vs. Will, Slave of James S. Battle. North Carolina Supreme Court, 1834.

The War of the Rebellion: A Compilation of the Official Records of the Union and Confederate Armies. Series 1, vol. 27, part 2. Washington, DC: Government Printing Office, 1889. RPT Historical Times, Inc., 1985.

Index

Made in the USA
Columbia, SC
11 June 2021